International Entrepreneurship as a Scholarly Field

Other titles in Foundations and Trends® in Entrepreneurship

Building Entrepreneurial Ecosystems Sustainably
Christina Theodoraki
ISBN: 978-1-63828-386-7

Generative AI in Entrepreneurship Research: Principles and Practical Guidance for Intelligence Augmentation
Francesco Ferrati, Phillip H. Kim and Moreno Muffatto
ISBN: 978-1-63828-384-3

Entrepreneurs' Search for Sources of Knowledge
Albert N. Link
ISBN: 978-1-63828-296-9

The Evolution of Hidden Champions as Niche Entrepreneurs
Erik E. Lehmann and Julian Schenkenhofer
ISBN: 978-1-63828-258-7

Entrepreneurship in the Long-Run: Empirical Evidence and Historical Mechanisms
Michael Fritsch and Michael Wyrwich
ISBN: 978-1-63828-108-5

Minority Entrepreneurship 2.0
Timothy Bates
ISBN: 978-1-63828-048-4

International Entrepreneurship as a Scholarly Field

Leo-Paul Dana
Dalhousie University
lp762359@dal.ca

Aidin Salamzadeh
University of Tehran
salamzadeh@ut.ac.ir

Boston — Delft

Foundations and Trends® in Entrepreneurship

Published, sold and distributed by:
now Publishers Inc.
PO Box 1024
Hanover, MA 02339
United States
Tel. +1-781-985-4510
www.nowpublishers.com
sales@nowpublishers.com

Outside North America:
now Publishers Inc.
PO Box 179
2600 AD Delft
The Netherlands
Tel. +31-6-51115274

The preferred citation for this publication is

L.-P. Dana and A. Salamzadeh. *International Entrepreneurship as a Scholarly Field*. Foundations and Trends® in Entrepreneurship, vol. 20, no. 7, pp. 679–780, 2024.

ISBN: 978-1-63828-458-1
© 2024 L.-P. Dana and A. Salamzadeh

All rights reserved. No part of this publication may be reproduced, stored in a retrieval system, or transmitted in any form or by any means, mechanical, photocopying, recording or otherwise, without prior written permission of the publishers.

Photocopying. In the USA: This journal is registered at the Copyright Clearance Center, Inc., 222 Rosewood Drive, Danvers, MA 01923. Authorization to photocopy items for internal or personal use, or the internal or personal use of specific clients, is granted by now Publishers Inc for users registered with the Copyright Clearance Center (CCC). The 'services' for users can be found on the internet at: www.copyright.com

For those organizations that have been granted a photocopy license, a separate system of payment has been arranged. Authorization does not extend to other kinds of copying, such as that for general distribution, for advertising or promotional purposes, for creating new collective works, or for resale. In the rest of the world: Permission to photocopy must be obtained from the copyright owner. Please apply to now Publishers Inc., PO Box 1024, Hanover, MA 02339, USA; Tel. +1 781 871 0245; www.nowpublishers.com; sales@nowpublishers.com

now Publishers Inc. has an exclusive license to publish this material worldwide. Permission to use this content must be obtained from the copyright license holder. Please apply to now Publishers, PO Box 179, 2600 AD Delft, The Netherlands, www.nowpublishers.com; e-mail: sales@nowpublishers.com

Foundations and Trends® in Entrepreneurship
Volume 20, Issue 7, 2024
Editorial Board

Editors-in-Chief

Albert N. Link
University of North Carolina at Greensboro
David B. Audretsch
Indiana University

Editors

Sophie Bacq
IMD Busiuness School

Maksim Belitski
University of Reading and Loyola University New Orleans

Daniel Bennett
University of Louisville

Rosa Caiazza
Parthenope University of Naples

Per Davidsson
Queensland University of Technology

Alfredo De Massis
D'Annunzio University and IMD Business School

Antje Fiedler
University of Auckland

Michael Frese
Asian School of Business

Brett Gilbert
American University

Maribel Guerrero
Arizona State University

Martin Kenney
University of California at Davis

Moren Levesque
York University

Jeff McMullen
Indiana University

Maria Minniti
Syracuse University

Boris Nikolaev
Colorado State University

Simon Parker
Western University

Pankaj C. Patel
Villanova University

Erik Stam
University of Utrecht

Christina Theodoraki
Aix-Marseille University

Roy Thurik
Erasmus University

Editorial Scope

Foundations and Trends® in Entrepreneurship publishes survey and tutorial articles in the following topics:

- Nascent and start-up entrepreneurs
- Opportunity recognition
- New venture creation process
- Business formation
- Firm ownership
- Market value and firm growth
- Franchising
- Managerial characteristics and behavior of entrepreneurs
- Strategic alliances and networks
- Government programs and public policy
- Gender and ethnicity

- New business financing:
    - Business angels
    - Bank financing, debt, and trade credit
    - Venture capital and private equity capital
    - Public equity and IPOs
- Family-owned firms
- Management structure, governance and performance
- Corporate entrepreneurship
- High technology:
    - Technology-based new firms
    - High-tech clusters
- Small business and economic growth

Information for Librarians

Foundations and Trends® in Entrepreneurship, 2024, Volume 20, 8 issues. ISSN paper version 1551-3114. ISSN online version 1551-3122. Also available as a combined paper and online subscription.

Contents

1 Introduction — 3
2 International Entrepreneurship (IE) — 7
3 Units of Analysis (Individual, Firm, Nation) — 13
4 Behavioural Factors in IE — 27
5 Structural Factors in IE — 39
6 Contextual Factors in IE — 49
7 Emerging Themes — 59
8 Toward the Future — 73

References — 87

International Entrepreneurship as a Scholarly Field

Leo-Paul Dana[1] and Aidin Salamzadeh[2]

[1] Dalhousie University, Canada, and LUT Business School, Finland; lp762359@dal.ca
[2] University of Tehran, Iran; salamzadeh@ut.ac.ir

ABSTRACT

This monograph presents a comprehensive framework for international entrepreneurship (IE). To make our contribution cohesive, first, we focus our attention on definitions; then, by providing an in-depth analysis of the impacts of both internal and external factors on the decision-making processes of entrepreneurs in the realm of IE, we elaborate on the implications within this domain. Moving beyond existing literature, we use a multi-level analysis. Within this framework, we scrutinize three fundamental units of analysis: the individual entrepreneur, the firm, and the country. It is posited that this approach will facilitate a comprehensive comprehension of the considerations pertinent to international entrepreneurship, along with the principal factors at each level of analysis. By encompassing all three levels, our objective is to illuminate the interconnectedness between individual traits, firm competencies, and national circumstances that shape international entrepreneurial activities.

Moreover, we adopt a behavioral perspective to scrutinize how international entrepreneurs perceive, evaluate, and capitalize on opportunities across borders. This lens enables us to acquaint our erudite audience with the decision-making procedures of these individuals. Consequently, this approach is expected to yield a more profound and nuanced insight into the motivations, risk assessments, and cognitive predispositions that shape the international entrepreneurial behavior of entrepreneurs. We believe this monograph will serve as a comprehensive and integrated resource for scholars and practitioners interested in international entrepreneurship.

1
Introduction

Entrepreneurship, characterized by dynamism and innovation, has transcended national borders through fostering innovation and economic growth across the globe. Furthermore, technological advancements have facilitated the internationalization of firms, regardless of size (Dana *et al.*, 1999b; Wright and Dana, 2003). Yet, from an academic perspective, entrepreneurship is a relatively new field (Landström, 2020) and international entrepreneurship is even newer. Dana (2017) explained the evolution of international entrepreneurship (IE); pioneer contributions in the field included McDougall (1989), and Dana and Wright (1997). Dana *et al.* (1999a) explained the theoretical foundations of the emerging field of IE. This was followed by McDougall and Oviatt (2000), Acs *et al.* (2003), Young *et al.* (2003) and Dana (2004). Dana and Wright (2009) identified priorities and their Delphi study was replicated by Etemad *et al.* (2022). This monograph sets the stage for a deeper understanding of the multifaceted phenomenon of IE.

Our contribution offers a comprehensive outlook of IE theoretical principles, empirical trends, and practical implications. By reviewing the prior studies on IE, we establish a historical context for the field. In this regard, we shift our focus from traditional, stage-based models of internationalization to a more comprehensive and adaptable one which includes "Born Globals" and "INVs". Following this, in Section 2, we explore the individual driving forces behind international ventures. We examine the unique characteristics, motivations, and competencies that distinguish international entrepreneurs from their domestic counterparts. We identify various factors such as cultural influences, risk tolerance, and global networks are among the key determinants of success in the international environment. Then, by recognizing the critical role of institutions in shaping the landscape for international ventures, in Section 3, we address the importance of formal institutions, such as legal systems and intellectual property rights. Consecutively, to make the subject more lucid, we demonstrate how these institutions can either facilitate or hinder international entrepreneurial activity.

In the next stage, in Section 4, we address the crucial role of the entrepreneurial ecosystem in nurturing and propelling international ventures. In this section, we highlight the various actors that contribute to the ecosystem and analyze how their support structures influence the internationalization process. To deepen our understanding, we center our attention on the practical considerations faced by entrepreneurial businesses venturing into foreign markets. In this section, we examine various entry mode strategies and analyze the factors influencing the choice of an appropriate strategy. Furthermore, in this section, we explore the challenges of managing international operations, including cultural adaptation and logistical complexities. Section 5 investigates a set of structural factors, such as inequality and institutions, related to IE. Then, in Section 6, we elaborate on the symbiotic relationship between innovation and international entrepreneurship. To do so, we acknowledge how internationalization can stimulate innovation by exposing ventures to new knowledge, markets, and resources. Conversely, in this section, we shed light on ways that innovation can be a key driver of internationalization, allowing ventures to develop unique products and services that hold global appeal.

Recognizing the role of government policies in fostering an environment conducive to international entrepreneurial activity is a subject that we address in Section 7. We also elucidate on various policy instruments that can encourage internationalization. Moreover, we highlight the challenges of balancing national interests with the demands of a globalized economy.

Our work concludes by addressing the emerging trends and challenges shaping the future of the field. In Section 8, we delve into the impact of technological advancements, such as e-commerce and digital platforms, on international market access and competition. Furthermore, in this section, we meticulously explain the growing importance of sustainability and social responsibility in the context of international entrepreneurship.

Thus, we intend to bridge the gap between theoretical frameworks and practical considerations. By drawing on insights from diverse research disciplines, including management, economics, and sociology, we attempt to offer a holistic understanding of this dynamic and ever-evolving field. The contribution is intended for a broad audience, encompassing scholars, students, policymakers, and practitioners alike.

2

International Entrepreneurship (IE)

Entrepreneurship has been considered as a motive force for the development of a country. The field of entrepreneurship has been introduced to help business people and entrepreneurs seek opportunities and solve their business-related problems in a more innovative and creative way. Entrepreneurship also improves the pace of business. Therefore, in a fast and ever-changing environment, this scholarly field can equip business people with great potential for success (Jafari-Sadeghi *et al.*, 2020b). Additionally, owing to the fact that entrepreneurship is based on the value creation, entrepreneurs do their best to maximize their performance. In this regard, entrepreneurs are expected to enhance their capabilities and in doing so gain a competitive edge over their rivals (Jafari-Sadeghi *et al.*, 2020b). In this regard, previous studies demonstrated that developing countries have great potential for entrepreneurial activities. Due to the point that the core principle of entrepreneurship is opportunity discovery and identification, entrepreneurs have a great chance to address a variety of problems in the context of developing countries. Therefore, in a comparison between developed and developing countries, it can be stated that, based on the opportunity for embarking on an entrepreneurial activity, developing countries have a greater potential

(Jafari-Sadeghi *et al.*, 2021). However, while the range of problems can be considered as a potential area for entrepreneurs to become involved in, developing countries are mostly grappling with many socio-economic problems such as poverty, high rates of unemployment, and a lack of proper institutional regulations.

Globalization – which we define as hyper-connectivity and homogenization of the world economy – has been taking place over the past few centuries. For instance, Adam Smith had his "vent for surplus" theory to explain why entrepreneurs would sell internationally; David Ricardo explained how comparative advantage makes trade mutually advantageous even if one country is more competitive in all production; Paul Krugman illustrated why geography and hence transport costs matter and why entrepreneurs with a large home market would do better in international markets; and Melitz asked how the macro-theories of trade apply on the level of heterogenous firms, pointing to the importance of firm productivity levels for entering into foreign markets. These insights underpin modern strategic trade policy and negotiations, tariff and international tax design, regional trade agreements, trade promotion efforts, and industrial policy.

What has happened in the past few decades is that the speed of globalization has greatly accelerated. In this regard, entrepreneurial firms have prepared themselves to comply with new *"rules of the game"*. These firms have to compete with rivals from around the globe (Lopes *et al.*, 2022). While this issue can be concerning, there is great potential for firms.

As we see it, the most important aspect of globalization today is that it opens up opportunity for cooperation (Dana *et al.*, 2000; Dana *et al.*, 2013; Etemad *et al.*, 2001; Wright and Dana, 2003). Indeed, firms must compete with companies from different countries and sizes (Wright and Dana, 2003), and competition is a hard task for them as some companies have a specific edge (e.g., resources and networks) that helps them to outmaneuver many business-related challenges and have a specific power in the highly competitive borderless business environment (Crespo *et al.*, 2024). However, it can bring about great benefits for firms active in this atmosphere as well. When facing fierce competition, these firms start to do their best and make internal and external evaluations to find inefficiencies in processes and operations (Sciascia *et al.*, 2012). This empowers them to not only gain a specific advantage in the global landscape, but also to improve the effectiveness, efficiency, and productivity of their businesses.

Whereas Sciascia *et al.* (2012) saw the intersection of entrepreneurship and international business as having set the stage for more agile and flexible presence of entrepreneurial firms in the international environment, we suggest that international entrepreneurship is at the intersection not only of entrepreneurship and international business, but also international economics, and preferably also geographical economics and geopolitics.

To formulate internationalization, Johanson and Vahlne (1977) in their international model of Uppsala posited that businesses aiming for internationalization have to undertake various actions starting from exporting and ending at establishment in the international environment. Johanson and Vahlne (1977) believed that businesses intend to extend their internally well-crafted knowledge into the business environment. This model which focused on step-by-step and gradual movement proved to be ineffective for entrepreneurial firms. However, the traditional model of internationalization, as proposed by Johanson and Vahlne (1977), might not be the most suitable approach for these resource-constrained entrepreneurial firms. This established model emphasizes a staged approach to internationalization, where firms progressively increase their international involvement, starting with low-risk options such as exporting and gradually transitioning to more complex modes like foreign direct investment. The model assumes a gradual accumulation of resources and capabilities over time, which allows firms to manage the increasing risks associated with deeper internationalization.

While this traditional model offers a valuable framework, entrepreneurial firms in developing economies often do not possess the essential capability to gradually build up. In their study, Oviatt and McDougall (1995) stated that there are various entrepreneurial firms that are working internationally but their model does not align with Uppsala. These authors believed that the internationalization process is, to some breath, specific for each firm regarding its size and stage of development (Jafari-Sadeghi *et al.*, 2020b). In this regard, they started to propound another model that is more suitable for entrepreneurs active in the international business environment. Therefore, based on McDougall and Oviatt (2000) international entrepreneurship "is a combination of innovative, proactive, and risk-seeking behaviours that crosses national borders and is intended to create value in organizations".

International entrepreneurship is a decision that can be affected by various factors. According to previous studies (i.e., Sciascia et al., 2012) these include both internal and external factors. Internal factors are those related to the inside of the organization or venture which comprise of human capital, key resources, and information. To elaborate, when a venture is dealing with many financial problems or having problems within its human resource structure, the internationalization decision may become hard for them. The reason is that when a venture aims at internationalization, it has to leverage all its internal resources to gain prosperity in the foreign market. The same is true for external factors. These factors, which are mostly related to the environment, are of great significance. In this regard, the institutional and contextual environment plays a crucial role (Nave and Ferreira, 2022). For instance, in an environment in which prevalent socio-cultural beliefs regarding women exist, a hostile and unpropitious setting would be hindering for this portion of society. Also, market saturation and market competition can be among the factors that affect entrepreneurship decisions in the international setting. To elaborate, when the market is saturated, firms may not be able to gain their expected profits. This issue, when coupled with various internal capabilities such as financial resources and accomplished human capital, can lead a firm to extend its venture to cross-border markets. Moreover, the fierce and ever-increasing competition in the home country can result in coming to this decision that *internationalization can be a suitable option*. In this regard, gaining insights into the internal and external factors can be of great significance for entrepreneurs intending to participate in international environments (Sciascia et al., 2012).

Entrepreneurs involved in the internationalization process may find the international environment a propitious solution for their problems inside their home country, since they would be able to expand their business into a new market where a new and wider range of customers are available. This paves the way for enterprises to gain more profit and extend their longevity (Nave and Ferreira, 2022). However, expanding business to the international markets is not without challenges. To be more specific, considering the fact that entrepreneurs have to engage in interacting with foreign markets, there may be various elements they are not aware of. In this regard, uncertainty in action rises. While some entrepreneurs may believe that the gain from this uncertainty is considerable, others may not be willing to involve themselves.

One key challenge related to entering international markets is the liability of foreignness. This liability is related to the specific disadvantages that new firms face when entering a new market. The liability of foreignness has some demonstrations among which we can enumerate the unfamiliarity with local regulations, consumer preferences, and distribution channels which can create hurdles for these firms. As a result, their efforts toward building strong brand recognition and trust with local stakeholders become a matter of further consideration. Additionally, psychic distance which refers to the perceived differences between a home and foreign market is considered as another problem that hinders international entrepreneurs. In particular, language, culture, and legal systems can make entrepreneurs feel a sense of remoteness. This feeling makes it difficult to accurately assess market opportunities and risks. Furthermore, managing complex logistics affairs in the international sphere can be considered as a problematic hurdle. Studies by Dana *et al.* (2022a,b) highlight the challenges of cross-border transportation, customs clearance, and managing a geographically dispersed supply chain. Delays, disruptions, and unexpected costs can significantly impact profitability. Another important factor is intellectual property. Protecting intellectual property (IP) rights in foreign markets can be an arduous and seemingly intricate process. Research by Dana (2007) suggests that weak enforcement mechanisms in some countries can expose entrepreneurs to the risk of counterfeiting and imitation. Another issue that has been a matter of scholarly attention in the past decade is political unrest, economic volatility, and currency fluctuations. These factors can deleteriously affect the international operations of a firm.

3

Units of Analysis (Individual, Firm, Nation)

As one of the most dynamic and influential fields in the global economy, international entrepreneurship significantly shapes the economic destiny of countries, companies, and individuals. This field deals with innovative and inclusive processes across geographical boundaries and has interested researchers and policymakers for decades. However, for a better and more complete understanding of the dynamics and complexities of international entrepreneurship, it is necessary to carefully examine different units of analysis, including the individual, the firm, and the nation.

The individual unit of analysis in international entrepreneurship is a powerful tool that examines the role of entrepreneurs as the primary agents of innovation and commercialization in global markets. These individuals, with their specific characteristics such as risk-taking, creativity, and the ability to understand market opportunities at the international level, are the driving force behind fundamental changes in global markets. Research at this level allows us to understand the cultural differences, personal experiences, and technical knowledge that shape the background of international entrepreneurs.

The firm unit of analysis is a multifaceted field that centers on companies aiming to broaden their activities to international markets. This level of analysis is instrumental in dissecting the strategies, structures, and business models companies employ to compete on a global scale. It also underscores the substantial influence of domestic and international politics on corporate decisions, adding a layer of intricacy to the field.

The national unit of analysis scrutinizes the role of countries and policy environments in forming entrepreneurship. This level of analysis is crucial in understanding the influence of laws, regulations, and support policies on entrepreneurial activities and international trade. Furthermore, these analyses can illuminate the impact of international relations and political and economic cooperation or conflicts on global entrepreneurship.

Investigating the interactions between these three levels of analysis units is particularly important. It's not just about understanding their impacts but also about the potential they hold when they interact. This understanding can help us design more optimal strategies for developing global entrepreneurship and identify new opportunities in this field, giving us hope for a brighter future in international entrepreneurship.

In this section, according to extensive case analysis, we will try to depict the dynamics between the individual, the company, and the nation in international entrepreneurship and provide solutions for advancing this field.

3.1 Individual Unit of Analysis in International Entrepreneurship

Analyzing and understanding the individual unit of analysis in international entrepreneurship allows us to identify and analyze entrepreneurs' strategies and examine more profound cultural, social, and technological influences in this process. By better understanding these dynamics, we can achieve new and more effective ways to support and promote international entrepreneurship, which ultimately leads to economic and social progress and development at the global level.

As one of the critical factors in the economic and social development of countries, international entrepreneurship is greatly influenced by individual decisions and behaviors (Jones and Casulli, 2014). The

3.1. Individual Unit of Analysis in International Entrepreneurship

personal level in this field focuses on entrepreneurs as the primary agents of innovation and entry into new markets (McDougall-Covin et al., 2014). Analyzing the environment in the individual dimension leads to a deeper understanding of the dynamic role of entrepreneurs in facing the uncertainties of international environments (Kiss et al., 2012). This entrepreneurship is recognized as a dynamic and challenging field that requires adaptation to different cultures, economic systems, and markets (Rialp et al., 2019).

International entrepreneurs must have specific personality traits, broad experiences, and international abilities to perform well in different environments (Zahra et al., 2014). Uncertainty tolerance, independence, and contingent intelligence are essential factors that help entrepreneurs provide innovative solutions in challenging situations and accept calculated risks (Etemad, 2015). The ability to plan and implement large projects is also one of the critical skills in international entrepreneurship (Knight and Liesch, 2016).

In addition to personality traits, entrepreneurs' educational and work experiences also play a significant role in their success (Alon et al., 2016). Education in different fields, such as business management, economics, or engineering, offers entrepreneurs a broader perspective and more diverse skills. This allows them to identify new opportunities in international markets (Cavusgil and Knight, 2015). Also, global experience, either studying or working in different countries, helps entrepreneurs to become more culturally adaptable (Autio et al., 2011).

The culture and socioeconomic environment in which entrepreneurs grow up also significantly affect their spirit and approach to entrepreneurship (Freeman et al., 2020). Childhood and adolescent experiences can play a role in forming entrepreneurial spirit. Entrepreneurs from families and communities promoting entrepreneurial values are more willing to take risks and innovate (Colli et al., 2013). Extensive networks of professional connections at the global level are also recognized as a critical factor in facilitating the entrepreneurial process and enhancing business performance at the international level (Prashantham and Dhanaraj, 2010). These networks include former colleagues, advisors, investors, and other entrepreneurs and help attract new resources, information, and opportunities (Zhou et al., 2024).

3.2 Entrepreneurs: Engines of Innovation in the Global Arena

Entrepreneurs at the international level are very effective in identifying and exploiting emerging opportunities with the knowledge and experience they gain from different markets. These individuals, who often have outstanding risk-taking and creative abilities, discover new markets and act as pioneers in entering these markets. By using their wide networks, they acquire resources and information to facilitate business processes, and these abilities are the foundation for great success in the international arena (Sedziniauskiene and Sekliuckiene, 2020; Shahid and Hallo, 2019).

Entrepreneurs in this network structure can take advantage of the many benefits of social capital. These benefits include communicative, cognitive, and structural aspects. International networking links technological capabilities and entrepreneurial tendencies with firms' export performance, especially in creative industries. This emphasizes that developing Internet technology and strengthening entrepreneurship are critical to creating wider international networks. Also, commitment to developing knowledge sharing, coordination, adaptation, and conflict resolution in networks can lead to unique interpersonal assets and improve firms' international performance in new international ventures. In addition, temporary international academic mobility can help increase entrepreneurs' entrepreneurial knowledge, in which the size of interpersonal social networks plays an important role, highlighting the importance of extensive international social networks for knowledge transfer and accumulation (Ripollés and Blesa, 2022; De Moortel *et al.*, 2021).

3.3 Behavioral Reasoning and Cultural Influences

International entrepreneurship requires an in-depth understanding of how culture influences the behavior of entrepreneurs. Entrepreneurs' contextual culture significantly impacts their attitude toward risk, innovation, and business methods. Also, self-efficacy as a psychological concept plays a vital role in the individual abilities of international entrepreneurs and helps them believe that they can succeed in complex, unstable, and uncertain environments. These beliefs not only shape their entrepreneurial behavior, but there is also the reverse, and the ecosystem of entrepreneurs will impact the institutional decision-making structure and affect national strategies and policies.

The integration of international business and entrepreneurship knowledge has expanded the limits of traditional views and emphasized the importance of understanding cultures in forming international entrepreneurial behaviors. By accepting and integrating these cultural influences, practitioners and policymakers can improve educational programs and strategies to guide and support entrepreneurs in dealing with the complexities of international entrepreneurship. These efforts help entrepreneurs better understand how different cultures interact in business and create new opportunities in global markets.

3.4 Individual Entrepreneurship and New Technologies

Individual entrepreneurship and new technologies have a high semantic affinity and continuous connection. In explaining this issue, we notice the influence of various factors that shape the behavior of entrepreneurs in the field of technology, including critical success factors (CSF) in empowering entrepreneurs to use technologies effectively to achieve success in their investments. Is. In addition, the role of cognitive factors related to information technology, such as computer self-efficacy and anxiety caused by the use of technology, is of high importance in forming entrepreneurial goals. These factors affect entrepreneurs' ability to use new technologies and play an essential role in forming technological views and innovative business models (Ács and Audretsch, 1991).

Studies show that individual factors such as employment status, income level, and perceived skills play a crucial role in entrepreneurship and its connection with technology, especially in fostering innovation-based economies. These factors directly affect the abilities and motivations of entrepreneurs to adopt and apply new technologies. Finally, it is essential to understand how entrepreneurial tendencies influence technology adoption. This understanding can help facilitate the adoption of new technologies in the workplace and increase productivity and innovation at the organizational level. Therefore, attention to this interaction between individual entrepreneurship and technological developments is significant for organizations and policymakers who seek to improve working conditions and foster innovation.

3.5 Firm Unit of Analysis in International Entrepreneurship

International entrepreneurial companies are entities that expand their activities beyond domestic borders and enter global levels. These companies usually offer their products or services internationally by utilizing innovations and advanced technologies. They seek a competitive advantage in global markets through creative strategies and strategic management. These companies, often called Born Global and International New Ventures, work proactively to identify and exploit global opportunities. They are usually young organizations with extensive knowledge and focus on developing innovative, technology-based products. Through their activities in several countries, these companies seek to gain a significant competitive advantage (Tarba and Almor, 2018; Clark and Pidduck, 2023).

International entrepreneurship refers to behaviors and activities focused on discovering, evaluating, and exploiting international opportunities. These activities strongly focus on opportunity-driven mechanisms that allow companies to emerge as key players in global markets. While entrepreneurs play an essential role in this process, some definitions focus more on the entrepreneurial approach at the firm level than on the individual. Collectively, international entrepreneurial firms are at the forefront of exploiting new technologies, developing global value chains, and taking advantage of market opportunities to establish themselves as driving forces in the international business landscape (Cieślik, 2017; Verbeke and Ciravegna, 2018).

In international entrepreneurship, firm analysis is one of the critical areas that examines the role of companies and organizations in developing and expanding business activities at the global level. These studies focus on organizational strategies, structures, and behaviors that enable companies to face new and diverse international markets (Kuratko, 2012). Corporate entrepreneurship in international business relies on developing a positive mindset and strategic planning, exploiting vast

3.6. Internationalization Strategies 19

financial and information resources to drive innovation and increase competitiveness. In this context, corporate social responsibility (CSR) also plays a prominent role, especially in industries such as insurance and banking, which affect companies' financial performance and interaction with stakeholders. Transnational Corporations (TNCs) also significantly affect the global economy through their activities, investments, and monopolies. These companies need effective management methods and advanced economic analysis techniques to manage challenges and continue their growth and sustainability (Ratten, 2022; Franco-Leal and Diaz-Carrion, 2022).

Also, the relationship between firm-level entrepreneurship and the international performance of firms, especially in small and medium-sized enterprises (SMEs), is influenced by several factors. These factors include entrepreneurial tendencies, environmental dynamics, and the ability to cooperate and build trust in business networks. Strengthening these aspects can help improve collective performance and international success, which indicates the increasing importance of collaboration and networking in modern business environments (Hosseini *et al.*, 2018).

3.6 Internationalization Strategies

International entrepreneurial companies adopt various strategies to achieve success in global markets. These strategies include developing new products, adapting to local cultures and demands, establishing effective distribution networks, and managing risk in volatile markets. Additionally, many companies strategically pursue international partnerships to facilitate access to new markets and benefit from joint ventures.

International strategies are particularly significant for enhancing international competitiveness and addressing global market challenges. Developing a critical international strategy is essential for companies to strengthen their competitive position. Born-digital companies with highly digital value chains emphasize the importance of digitalization in their internationalization strategies.

Decision-making in internationalization strategies involves dealing with uncertainties and considering different models, such as the OLI paradigm and the global decision-making approach. Moreover, the role of international entrepreneurial orientation and specific strategies in SMEs from developing countries, such as Indian companies producing personal protective equipment, underscores the importance of commitment to quality and innovation in international growth (Annushkina and Regazzo, 2020; Audretsch and Lehmann, 2011; Dewan and Singh, 2019; Zhang et al., 2019).

Companies face numerous challenges when implementing global entrepreneurship initiatives, including adapting to global market competition, economic issues, ICT challenges, and the need to understand the diverse cultural perspectives of internal and external stakeholders. They must also manage international financial, technological, social, and legal issues when conducting e-commerce globally. Balancing global and local needs, controlling and coordinating diverse units worldwide, and reaping the benefits of international operations are constantly under review. Additionally, to face the legitimacy challenges in implementing corporate social responsibility, companies should align CSR initiatives with their business model and effectively present their CSR philosophy to gain stakeholders' legitimacy. These multifaceted challenges require strategic decision-making, solid management approaches, and a deep understanding of global dynamics to successfully guide global entrepreneurship initiatives (Li and Gammelgaard, 2014; Zhang et al., 2019; Zhu et al., 2014).

Market trends play an important role in shaping internationalization strategies in corporate entrepreneurship. Entering international markets is affected by uncertainty, consumer demand, foreign laws, and competition. Effective international expansion includes systematically expanding organizational processes, conducting strategic analysis, and developing a strategic plan. Furthermore, integrating concepts such as corporate entrepreneurship, host country institutions, and regulatory focus into an integrated framework helps explain the firm internationalization process. It highlights the importance of pre-entry strategies for successful international ventures. Additionally, the research emphasizes the positive effect of corporate entrepreneurship on the internationalization of small and medium-sized enterprises, which, especially for smaller enterprises, serves as an effective way to increase competitive advantage and market presence (Park *et al.*, 2021; Pucik *et al.*, 2023; Werhane, 2012).

As a result, the firm level of analysis in international entrepreneurship provides essential insights into how companies form and implement international strategies. Understanding these strategies and their associated challenges is crucial to success in the global arena. Using these perspectives, companies can compete more effectively in global markets and realize their full potential in the international arena.

3.7 The National Level of Analysis in International Entrepreneurship

The national level of analysis in international entrepreneurship examines the role of governments and macro policies in developing and forming entrepreneurial activities at the global level. These analyses show how the legal, economic, and political environments affect entrepreneurs and firms and explain how governments can promote or constrain international entrepreneurship. This level of analysis is critical for understanding the impact of institutional conditions, supportive policies, and country-specific factors on entrepreneurship. Institutional conditions at the national level play an important role in facilitating or limiting the internationalization efforts of entrepreneurs in the early stages. Entrepreneurs operating in the international arena face different challenges and opportunities than their domestic counterparts and emphasize the importance of careful analysis of national policies and frameworks. Additionally, macroeconomic indicators and the national entrepreneurship system influence entrepreneurship at the national level, stressing the need to prioritize the development of support frameworks for entrepreneurs. Understanding contextual factors at the national level, such as regulatory quality, innovation systems, and market size, is necessary to promote and strengthen international entrepreneurial activities in different countries (Singh and Majumdar, 2020; Muralidharan and Pathak, 2020).

Domestic policies of a country can have significant effects on international activities. For example, supportive policies that strengthen the technology and innovation sectors can lead to the development of competitive products and services in global markets. Conversely, contractionary policies that impose strict restrictions on economic activities can hinder companies' growth and international expansion. A thorough understanding of local regulations is critical to global entrepreneurship, as it helps reduce barriers to foreign investment and ensures compliance with labor laws and financial regulations. Local laws, such as China's labor standards and US financial regulations, play an essential role in the global economy, affecting economic well-being and power dynamics between political and economic actors. By understanding and adhering to these regulations, employers can fill legal gaps, set legal standards, meet their obligations under labor law, employee rights and benefits, and data protection. This understanding not only helps to create better relations with local governments but also helps to avoid legal conflicts and ultimately contributes to the success and sustainability of international entrepreneurial investments (Danielsen, 2010; Chowdhury and Audretsch, 2021).

3.8 The Effect of Government Policies on International Entrepreneurship

Governments directly impact the entrepreneurial environment through policies and programs, such as tax laws, import and export regulations, and financial support. These policies can act as drivers for entrepreneurship development or put obstacles in the way of entrepreneurs. For example, encouraging tax policies can motivate companies to invest and innovate more, while cumbersome laws can slow down the entrepreneurial process (Cumming et al., 2009; Audretsch et al., 2005).

Governments can help facilitate international trade by building appropriate infrastructure and providing the necessary facilities, such as advanced information and communication technologies. Additionally, bilateral or multilateral trade agreements can reduce trade barriers and increase companies' access to new markets. These measures not only help reduce business costs but also accelerate the international expansion of companies. By creating supportive business environments, governments can help strengthen the foundations of entrepreneurship and promote innovation. Support programs can include financial grants, awarding research grants, and providing advice and guidance to entrepreneurs. These programs help entrepreneurs develop innovative ideas and compete in global markets (Chang *et al.*, 2017; Ajayi-Nifise *et al.*, 2024).

One of the main challenges entrepreneurs face at the national level is legal and bureaucratic obstacles that can slow down or even stop business development. Complex and time-consuming laws, lengthy processes for registering companies and obtaining the necessary permits, and the lack of legal clarity can all act as severe barriers to entrepreneurship. Governments should seek to remove these obstacles and create a transparent and efficient legal environment to help facilitate entrepreneurial activities (Mehrez, 2019; Lerner, 2002).

3.9 Challenges and Opportunities of National Unit of Analysis in International Entrepreneurship

The national unit of analysis in international entrepreneurship encompasses understanding the impact of governments and macroeconomic policies on entrepreneurial processes. This sector plays a vital role in determining the path of economic development and global business opportunities. In this text, the challenges and opportunities that the national unit of analysis creates for entrepreneurs and companies active in the international arena are discussed in depth.

3.9.1 Challenges

(1) Cumbersome Regulations: One of the biggest challenges for entrepreneurs and companies is the strict and complex government regulations that can slow the entrepreneurial process. These regulations include necessary licenses to start a business, tax laws, and business standards, which are sometimes very difficult and time-consuming.

(2) Limited Support Policies: In some countries, the lack of sufficient support policies for the development of entrepreneurship, especially on an international scale, can be a significant obstacle to the development of foreign markets. Lack of financial resources,

training programs, and necessary support to explore new markets contribute to these challenges.

(3) Political Changes and Instability: Political instability and sudden changes in government policies can threaten the long-term plans of entrepreneurs and companies. These changes can include changes in tax laws, export and import laws, and other regulatory laws that affect the business environment.

3.9.2 Opportunities

(1) Government Incentive Policies: Governments can create a favorable environment for international entrepreneurship through incentive policies such as tax exemptions, financial aid, and investment in infrastructure. These policies can help entrepreneurs quickly enter new markets by reducing monetary risk and providing access to necessary resources.

(2) Support and Training Programs: Through support and training programs, governments can strengthen entrepreneurs and companies in technology, international management, and marketing strategies. These programs can include workshops, seminars, and training courses that provide the necessary knowledge and skills to compete in global markets.

(3) International Trade Agreements: Governments can reduce trade barriers and increase companies' access to global markets by establishing and strengthening bilateral and multilateral trade agreements. These agreements can help facilitate exports and imports and create new business growth and development opportunities.

The national unit of analysis in international entrepreneurship can source countless challenges and opportunities. By adopting prudent and supportive policies, governments can help facilitate international entrepreneurship and create an environment where entrepreneurs and companies can compete successfully in global markets. Considering these challenges and opportunities, entrepreneurs and policymakers can design and implement more optimal strategies for developing international entrepreneurship.

3.10 Interactions Between Levels in International Entrepreneurship

As a complex and multifaceted process, international entrepreneurship is influenced by interlevel interactions between individuals, companies, and governments. These interactions at each analytical level significantly shape the opportunities and challenges in international entrepreneurship. Examining these interactions can lead to a better understanding of the dynamics of the global entrepreneurial environment and how to navigate them.

3.11 Interaction Between Entrepreneurs and Companies

Entrepreneurs, as driving forces who identify and seize international opportunities, play a crucial role in defining the direction and strategies of companies. By leveraging their individual knowledge and global experiences, they often act as bridges that connect companies to new markets. Conversely, companies empower entrepreneurs to achieve international goals by providing resources, knowledge, and organizational structures. This reciprocal interaction between individuals and companies fundamentally determines the success of entrepreneurs in the global arena.

3.12 Interaction Between Companies and Governments

Companies operate within national legal and economic environments shaped by governments. By establishing regulations, tax policies, and trade agreements, governments can create environments that either facilitate or hinder the flourishing of international business activities. Successful companies in the global arena can enhance national incomes and improve their countries' global standing, providing economic and political benefits to governments.

3.13 Interaction Between Entrepreneurs and Governments

International entrepreneurs directly impact local and global economies and can serve as cultural and economic ambassadors for their countries. Demonstrating their individual and entrepreneurial capabilities can influence policymakers' perspectives and reinforce supportive policies. This mutual interaction between individuals and governments can lead to a positive innovation and economic growth cycle.

Interlevel interactions in international entrepreneurship are central to shaping opportunities and addressing challenges. Understanding and utilizing these interactions can help entrepreneurs and policymakers design and implement more optimal strategies for developing and expanding entrepreneurial activities at the international level. Therefore, a detailed and profound understanding of these interactions is essential for formulating policies and programs that support and guide entrepreneurial processes at various levels.

4

Behavioural Factors in IE

International Entrepreneurship (IE) is recognized as a dynamic and multidimensional domain where entrepreneurs leverage global opportunities to extend their innovative activities beyond national boundaries. This domain integrates entrepreneurship and internationalization, explores how entrepreneurs cultivate new markets, and delves into the behavioral factors influencing their decisions and strategies. The behavior of international entrepreneurs, encompassing how they discover, evaluate, and exploit entrepreneurial opportunities, will be scrutinized in depth in this section.

As a dynamic environment, international entrepreneurship necessitates understanding entrepreneurial behaviors, particularly how entrepreneurs respond to potential international opportunities and how these behaviors translate into significant business ventures. Therefore, analyzing the behaviors that propel entrepreneurs towards international markets is crucial. Factors such as entrepreneurs' risk-taking, innovation, and personal motivations are essential as they determine the discovery and exploitation of new opportunities. Specifically, risk-taking, the propensity to invest in high-potential but uncertain outcomes, is pivotal in international entrepreneurship. This attribute enables entrepreneurs to transcend traditional safety boundaries and undertake risks in unfamiliar markets. Besides risk-taking, innovation is also acknowledged as a critical driver of international entrepreneurship. Innovation manifests in products and services, market approaches, and business strategies. Entrepreneurs capable of providing creative and practical solutions to existing problems are more adept at attracting and retaining customers in international markets.

Alongside risk-taking and innovation, personal motivations are significant in international entrepreneurship. These motivations may include the desire for personal growth, achieving financial independence, or making a social impact. These motivations help entrepreneurs endure challenges and persist in achieving their long-term goals. Furthermore, entrepreneurs' social and professional networks are not just crucial, but they are the backbone of facilitating international entrepreneurship. These networks offer valuable resources such as information, advice, financial support, and business opportunities, which can mitigate the risks associated with entering new markets. Consequently, developing and maintaining robust networks can help entrepreneurs swiftly establish and succeed in international markets, providing a sense of reassurance and support.

In this section, we aim to comprehensively understand the behavioral factors in international entrepreneurship to enhance our grasp of how entrepreneurs engage with global opportunities and their challenges. This analysis will enable us to identify more effective strategies to support entrepreneurs in the internationalization process and bolster their capabilities to compete globally.

4.1 Entrepreneurs and Risk-Taking in International Opportunities

Risk-taking is a pivotal element in international entrepreneurship, acting as a driving force for companies that venture beyond their domestic markets. This analysis synthesizes findings from the presented literature to examine how risk-taking influences pursuing international opportunities. It highlights the subtle impacts of varying risk engagement levels on a firm's success in global markets. Risk tolerance in international entrepreneurship refers to a firm's willingness to engage in ventures

4.1. Entrepreneurs and Risk-Taking in International Opportunities

with uncertain outcomes. This may encompass entering new markets characterized by different cultural, regulatory, and economic environments. Studies indicate that risk tolerance is multi-dimensional, with its degree and impact varying significantly depending on the company's strategy and market conditions (Dai *et al.*, 2014).

Moderate levels of risk-taking are often more effective than extreme positions. Firms engaging in moderate risk-taking are more likely to achieve broader international reach than those overly cautious or excessively bold. This balanced approach allows companies to balance acquiring new opportunities, managing potential losses, and optimizing their international development efforts (Guo and Jiang, 2020). In much of the internationalization literature, high risk and uncertainty are regarded as constraints on progress. However, it is posited that risk-taking can both catalyze and impede international operations. On the one hand, it drives companies towards pioneering innovations, entering new markets, and potentially receiving higher rewards. On the other hand, excessive risk-taking can lead to overcommitment of resources and possible failures, especially if risks are not well-managed or aligned with the firm's capabilities and market realities (Welch and Luostarinen, 1988).

Previous international experiences have shown that they increase individuals' risk tolerance. Those with experience working and living in international environments tend to demonstrate higher levels of open-mindedness and flexibility. Additionally, individuals with high-level occupations and education, often due to exposure to global settings, require higher risk tolerance to become successful entrepreneurs. Exposure to diverse cultures and work environments can enhance a person's willingness to take risks, as these experiences foster adaptability and broaden perspectives. Thus, there is a direct correlation between international experiences and risk tolerance, underscoring the importance of examining these factors to understand entrepreneurial behavior and decision-making (Fuentelsaz *et al.*, 2022; Genkova, 2016).

4.2 Strategic Implications of Risk-Taking

The strategic implementation of risk-taking must be carefully managed. Companies need to evaluate their resource bases, market conditions, and competitive prospects to determine the appropriate level of risk-taking. Studies indicate that companies benefit from adopting a balanced approach, where risks are neither avoided nor pursued unthinkingly. This balance is crucial in navigating the complexities of international markets and achieving sustainable growth. International entrepreneurs who engage in risk-taking behaviors strategically position themselves for success in global markets. Research suggests that small and medium-sized enterprises (SMEs) consciously target high-risk markets to gain local legitimacy, reflecting a smart risk-taking strategy that aids their success abroad. By accepting calculated risks, these companies can enter new markets and secure competitive positions, significantly contributing to their growth and development (Dominguez and Raïs, 2012).

CEOs inclined to take higher risks tend to lead their companies toward bolder internationalization decisions. These decisions often involve entering countries with substantial cultural differences and employing riskier entry methods, such as direct acquisitions. By understanding and managing risks wisely, these managers can identify and exploit more opportunities in international markets (Boustanifar *et al.*, 2022).

Moreover, companies in emerging economies, like the Indian pharmaceutical industry, exhibit entrepreneurial behavior essential for managing the intense risks associated with global competition. These companies strive to attain a stable competitive position in advanced international markets by adopting innovative and entrepreneurial approaches. Strategic entrepreneurship is vital for success in global markets characterized by multiple risks and competitive challenges (Ramachandran *et al.*, 2006).

Intelligence risk-taking and its strategic application can guide companies toward international growth and success. Companies that approach risk consciously and calculatedly, rather than avoiding it, can exploit opportunities arising from risk and achieve success in new markets. This approach helps businesses remain competitive in international environments and enables them to leverage existing challenges and uncertainties.

Research findings demonstrate that strategic risk-taking can drive international entrepreneurial ventures toward growth and success. Managers should exploit risk wisely instead of avoiding it to succeed in complex and dynamic global markets. This strategy enables them to overcome challenges and use existing opportunities best. Consequently, intelligent and strategic risk-taking can be critical to a company's success and international growth (Liesch *et al.*, 2011; Busenitz, 1999).

Given the importance of risk-taking in the internationalization process, companies should develop comprehensive strategies for risk management. This includes thorough market analysis, identifying opportunities and threats, and designing reactive plans to tackle challenges. Additionally, developing managerial skills and capabilities to manage international risks can enhance company performance. The ability to accept and manage global risks, particularly in challenging markets, allows companies to innovate and maintain their competitive position continuously. This approach promotes companies' growth and development, generating added value for all stakeholders. Thus, intelligent and strategic risk-taking can determine companies' long-term success and sustainability in the international arena.

4.3 Innovation in International Entrepreneurship

Innovation and entrepreneurship are two critical elements that are deeply intertwined and essential for the growth and success of businesses in today's globalized economy. The field of international entrepreneurship (IE), which explores the dynamics between these two elements, illustrates how firms can leverage their innovative capabilities to enter and thrive in global markets. This interaction not only aids companies in competing globally but also enables them to experience significant growth and markedly improve their performance. The ability to innovate within international entrepreneurship plays a pivotal role in creating and developing new market opportunities. Innovation involves generating new ideas and solutions, including developing novel products, discovering uncharted markets, or creating revolutionary business models. This creative process allows companies to distinguish themselves from competitors and establish a strong brand presence in the global market.

Moreover, innovation enables companies to respond more swiftly to market changes and maintain their position as industry leaders.

Understanding the impact of innovation on internationalization necessitates examining how companies interact with diverse cultures and markets. Innovation can assist companies in understanding different cultures and customizing their products or services to meet local needs. This level of cultural adaptation facilitates better acceptance of products in new markets and allows companies to build a sustainable customer base by fostering customer trust and loyalty. Additionally, innovation in international entrepreneurship entails adopting advanced technologies and digital tools that can enhance business processes and increase operational efficiency. Utilizing new technologies such as artificial intelligence, big data analytics, and cloud platforms helps companies collect, analyze, and use data more effectively. This not only aids in optimizing strategic decision-making but also enables companies to react more swiftly to market opportunities and engage in global competition.

Innovation is a continuous process that demands a commitment to ongoing learning and development. International entrepreneurs seeking innovation must cultivate organizational cultures emphasizing excellence, creativity, and risk-taking. Developing such a culture helps companies remain industry leaders, explore new markets, and achieve significant success on the global stage (Hagen *et al.*, 2014; O'Cass and Weerawardena, 2009).

However, the causal relationship between these two aspects remains contentious. Some studies indicate a strong link between them, while others do not corroborate this connection. These discrepancies in research findings may arise from differences in research methodologies, market conditions, and the variables under investigation. To clarify this issue, it is essential to recognize that numerous factors can influence study results. For instance, industry type, company size, financial and human resources access, and cultural and economic differences between countries can significantly shape outcomes. Furthermore, the type and quality of innovations examined can also impact the relationship between innovation and success in international markets. Some innovations may have an immediate and direct effect on company performance, while others may require more time to manifest their impact.

More comprehensive studies with robust methodologies and consideration of various variables are necessary to understand these complexities better. Such studies can help elucidate the causal relationship between innovation and success in international markets and provide more practical and precise guidance for entrepreneurs (Hagen *et al.*, 2014).

4.4 The Necessity of Studying Innovation in Non-High-Tech Sectors

To date, the majority of research in the field of innovation and international entrepreneurship has focused on high-tech industries. This emphasis is due to these industries' dynamic and rapidly changing nature, which provides numerous opportunities for innovation. However, non-high-tech industries also require innovation to remain competitive in global markets. These industries include sectors such as traditional manufacturing, agriculture, services, and tourism, each facing unique challenges and opportunities. Innovation in these sectors can manifest in various forms. For example, improving production processes, offering new services, utilizing new marketing methods, or even changing business models can help companies succeed in international markets. A deeper understanding of these innovations can lead to developing more effective strategies to support businesses in these industries.

Another area that necessitates further research is immigrant entrepreneurship. Immigrants often encounter numerous challenges, such as limited resource access, cultural differences, and language barriers. Nevertheless, this group of entrepreneurs also possesses a high innovation potential. Research indicates that immigrants frequently view the market with new and different perspectives, which can lead to unique innovations. Innovation in immigrant entrepreneurship may include developing products and services that cater to the specific needs of immigrant communities or leveraging social and business networks to create new opportunities. Furthermore, immigrants may draw upon their experiences from their home countries to develop new and efficient business models. A better understanding of these innovations can facilitate enhanced support for immigrant entrepreneurs and increase their chances of success in international markets (Keupp and Gassmann, 2009; Peiris *et al.*, 2012).

4.5 Entrepreneurial Orientation and Open Innovation in the Internationalization of Companies and Economic Development

Entrepreneurial orientation, characterized by innovation, proactivity, and risk-taking, significantly influences a company's internationalization ability. Firms with a strong entrepreneurial orientation tend to perform better in international markets (Dai *et al.*, 2014). Open innovation involves collaboration with external partners and is critical for global entrepreneurship. This approach enables companies to address business challenges and societal needs effectively while expanding their international reach. Cooperation with external partners can include participation in research and development, sharing resources, or collaboration in production and marketing. Such partnerships allow companies to benefit from diverse knowledge and experiences, elevating their innovations to new heights. For example, by collaborating with a local partner in a foreign market, a company can more effectively market its products and gain customer trust (Ziyae and Zali, 2017; Sullivan Mort and Weerawardena, 2006).

Entrepreneurial innovation significantly contributes to economic development, particularly in developing countries. Institutional environments play a crucial role in shaping the impact of innovative activities on economic growth. These institutions can include supportive laws and regulations, access to financial and educational resources, and adequate infrastructure. The presence of these institutions helps entrepreneurs engage in innovative activities with greater confidence and reduces the risks associated with internationalization (Szirmai *et al.*, 2011).

4.6 Innovation in International Entrepreneurship

Innovation and entrepreneurship are two critical elements that are deeply intertwined and essential for the growth and success of businesses in today's globalized economy. The field of international entrepreneurship (IE), which explores the dynamics between these two elements,

4.6. Innovation in International Entrepreneurship

illustrates how firms can leverage their innovative capabilities to enter and thrive in global markets. This interaction not only aids companies in competing globally but also enables them to experience significant growth and markedly improve their performance. The ability to innovate within international entrepreneurship plays a pivotal role in creating and developing new market opportunities. Innovation involves generating new ideas and solutions, including developing novel products, discovering uncharted markets, or creating revolutionary business models. This creative process allows companies to distinguish themselves from competitors and establish a strong brand presence in the global market. Moreover, innovation enables companies to respond more swiftly to market changes and maintain their position as industry leaders.

Understanding the impact of innovation on internationalization necessitates examining how companies interact with diverse cultures and markets. Innovation can assist companies in understanding different cultures and customizing their products or services to meet local needs. This level of cultural adaptation facilitates better acceptance of products in new markets and allows companies to build a sustainable customer base by fostering customer trust and loyalty. Additionally, innovation in international entrepreneurship entails adopting advanced technologies and digital tools that can enhance business processes and increase operational efficiency. Utilizing new technologies such as artificial intelligence, big data analytics, and cloud platforms helps companies collect, analyze, and use data more effectively. This not only aids in optimizing strategic decision-making but also enables companies to react more swiftly to market opportunities and engage in global competition.

Innovation is a continuous process that demands a commitment to ongoing learning and development. International entrepreneurs seeking innovation must cultivate organizational cultures emphasizing excellence, creativity, and risk-taking. Developing such a culture helps companies remain industry leaders, explore new markets, and achieve significant success on the global stage (Hagen *et al.*, 2014; O'Cass and Weerawardena, 2009).

However, the causal relationship between these two aspects remains contentious. Some studies indicate a strong link between them, while others do not corroborate this connection. These discrepancies in research findings may arise from differences in research methodologies, market conditions, and the variables under investigation. To clarify this issue, it is essential to recognize that numerous factors can influence study results. For instance, industry type, company size, financial and human resources access, and cultural and economic differences between countries can significantly shape outcomes. Furthermore, the type and quality of innovations examined can also impact the relationship between innovation and success in international markets. Some innovations may have an immediate and direct effect on company performance, while others may require more time to manifest their impact.

More comprehensive studies with robust methodologies and consideration of various variables are necessary to understand these complexities better. Such studies can help elucidate the causal relationship between innovation and success in international markets and provide more practical and precise guidance for entrepreneurs (Hagen *et al.*, 2014).

4.7 Personal Motivations of Entrepreneurs in International Entrepreneurship

Personal motivations are essential in the entrepreneurial journey, especially in international entrepreneurship. These motivations can act as drivers that lead entrepreneurs to search for and take advantage of new opportunities in global markets. In this work, we examine the detailed and scientific impact of personal motivations on the path of international entrepreneurship.

- Achievement and Power: Personal values such as achievement, power, self-direction, philanthropy, and security drive entrepreneurs to pursue international opportunities (Bolzani and Foo, 2018). These values act as cognitive frameworks that shape their internationalization goals.

- Independence and Recognition: Entrepreneurs are often driven by the desire for independence, achievement, recognition, sociability, and financial success. These motivations cross cultural boundaries,

4.7. Personal Motivations of Entrepreneurs

although they may appear differently in various socio-economic environments (Blais and Toulouse, 1990).

- Cultural and Social Influences: Cultural and social contexts, such as nationality and cultural norms, influence entrepreneurial motivations. For example, Chinese transnational entrepreneurs are motivated by entrepreneurial perspectives and cultural adaptation in their home and host countries (Dimitratos *et al.*, 2016).

- Opportunity Recognition: Opportunity-based entrepreneurship is influenced by personal characteristics such as entrepreneurial self-efficacy and the ability to recognize and exploit opportunities, often facilitated by supportive institutions in home countries (Yang *et al.*, 2020a,b).

- Economic and Social Drivers: In developing economies, drivers include necessity, poverty reduction, job creation, and personal knowledge and experience. Entrepreneurs also use entrepreneurial networks and competitive markets, although they face challenges such as lack of finance and political instability (Kah *et al.*, 2022).

Personal motivations play a vital role in the path of international entrepreneurship. These motivations drive entrepreneurs to seek and take advantage of new opportunities in global markets. These motivations influence strategic decisions, cultural adaptation, development of international networks, and management of artistic challenges. By understanding and strengthening these motivations, entrepreneurs can have a more successful path in the global arena and contribute to countries' economic growth and development.

To better understand the influence of behavioral factors in international entrepreneurship, this section explores the role of personal motivation, innovation, and risk-taking in the journey of global entrepreneurs. International entrepreneurship offers more significant and diverse business opportunities and presents challenges and obstacles, necessitating a detailed understanding of critical entrepreneurial behaviors.

Personal motivations serve as powerful drivers that propel entrepreneurs toward global opportunities. These motivations, which may include the desire for independence, achieving financial success, or creating social impact, play a crucial role in shaping entrepreneurs' international strategies and decisions. Innovation, another significant focus of this section, is recognized as a fundamental pillar in the development and growth of businesses on a global scale. Innovation is essential not only in products and services but also in market approaches and strategies. Entrepreneurs who provide creative and effective solutions can gain a more decisive competitive advantage in international markets. Risk-taking is also highlighted as one of the most essential characteristics of global entrepreneurs. The ability to manage risk and make decisions under uncertainty enables entrepreneurs to identify and effectively exploit new opportunities. Moderate risk-taking, in particular, can allow businesses to expand more successfully and sustainably in global markets.

In conclusion, this section emphasizes that combining solid personal motivations, continuous innovation, and intelligent risk management can guide entrepreneurs toward success in international markets. By implementing strategies based on these factors, entrepreneurs can enhance their impact on the global stage and contribute to countries' economic and social development. This section invites a deeper understanding and optimal utilization of entrepreneurial capabilities worldwide, potentially leading to a brighter future for international businesses.

5

Structural Factors in IE

The global business environment is characterized by dynamism and opportunity. However, this is mixed with a form of inequality and unpropitious institutional farces. Of course inequality is nothing new. Thomas Piketty demonstrated in his *magnum opus* that inequality in today's world has deep historical roots. Partly, these roots lie in centuries of imperialism and colonialism, driven by international entrepreneurs, e.g., the creation of the world's first multinational, the *Dutch Verenigde Oostindische Compagnie* or United East India Company in 1602 as heralding in a period of colonial conquest and exploitation (Dana, 2018). In Marxian analyses, the search for never-ending growth and profit by firms lead them to expand into adjacent countries and domains, until all potential for consumption and production growth is exhausted, as explained in the 1913 thesis of Rosa Luxemburg. Social justice today requires that international entrepreneurs be sensitised as to the history behind international venturing, and that they be aware of the deep structural inequalities as legacies of this domination.

Various factors in a country can influence entrepreneurship. For instance, in developing countries, firms mostly have to deal with various institutional problems and exert energy to surmount these obstacles.

While some of these obstacles are problematic for most firms, other firms may not be impacted by these barriers (Jafari-Sadeghi *et al.*, 2020b). Entrepreneurial firms in developing economies, while playing a pivotal role in driving economic growth and fostering local development, face a multitude of challenges that their counterparts in developed economies often do not. This disparity, added to the cumbersome institutional factors, creates an uneven playing field, hindering entrepreneurial firms active in a country to compete effectively. Therefore, limited access to crucial resources, the specter of economic sanctions, and inadequate infrastructural development form a triumvirate of obstacles that can stifle their entrepreneurial spirit (Luo and Bu, 2018b). In this regard, these entrepreneurial firms may adopt various strategies to first survive and reach viability, and then seek prosperity and thrive. Among these strategies, internationalization ranks near the top. Nevertheless, before going any further, we first intend to elucidate on the relationship between inequality and international entrepreneurship.

5.1 Inequality and International Entrepreneurship

Inequality is a highly debated concept in various academic fields such as politics, philosophy, and sociology, as evidenced by the works of Bruton *et al.* (2021) and Packard and Bylund (2018). Within this discourse, some scholars perceive inequality as a negative force that creates social stratification, while others contend that it serves as a catalyst for progress and advancement in societies. Scholars who take the former stance argue that inequality poses a significant challenge to a nation's capacity to establish a fair and just environment with equal opportunities for all individuals. They posit that extensive inequality, incorporating elements like inadequate education, restricted access to resources, and decreased consumption levels, can undermine the overall well-being and prosperity of a country, as demonstrated by Aceytuno *et al.* (2020) and Bruton *et al.* (2021). Moreover, they assert that such inequality may foster socio-political unrest, as highlighted by Aceytuno *et al.* (2020). Conversely, other researchers assert that inequality is an inherent aspect of human society, an argument supported by Lippmann *et al.* (2005) and Packard and Bylund (2018). These studies suggest that

5.1. Inequality and International Entrepreneurship

inequality plays a vital role in promoting economic growth and ensuring national stability, as indicated by Gabaix *et al.* (2016) and Packard and Bylund (2018). Advocates of this perspective maintain that unequal access to resources and various personal attributes within markets and societies is essential for a country's progress and overall success. This ongoing debate also extends to the realm of entrepreneurship, as noted by Aceytuno *et al.* (2020).

Some researchers contend that there is a positive relationship between entrepreneurship and inequality. According to this viewpoint, entrepreneurship, traditionally perceived as a male-dominated domain, inherently embodies inequality, a notion supported by Vracheva and Stoyneva (2020) and Gupta *et al.* (2009). This perspective is rooted in socio-cultural norms and gender stereotypes that prevail not only in most societies but also within the entrepreneurial sphere, as discussed by previous scholars (Cowden *et al.*, 2023; Javadian *et al.*, 2021; Simarasl *et al.*, 2022). Previous studies on gender and entrepreneurship have suggested that women possess traits such as compassion, kindness, and risk aversion that are seemingly at odds with the characteristics typically associated with entrepreneurship, as highlighted by Cowden *et al.* (2023) and Gupta *et al.* (2014). In contrast, entrepreneurship has been characterized by qualities like assertiveness, aggressiveness, competitiveness, and a willingness to take risks, as emphasized by Cowden *et al.* (2023) and Javadian *et al.* (2021). Furthermore, entrepreneurs from geographically distant regions face numerous challenges, such as limited access to education, resources, and reliable networks, which can hinder their entrepreneurial aspirations, as pointed out by Bachmann *et al.* (2024), Kelly and McAdam (2022), and Ratten *et al.* (2019).

Moreover, the process of acquiring resources, a crucial step for aspiring entrepreneurs, presents significant obstacles, as traditional investors and financial institutions often prefer to support more established businesses. However, an opposing viewpoint suggests a negative relationship between inequality and entrepreneurship, as argued by Bruton *et al.* (2021), Halvarsson *et al.* (2018), and Lippmann *et al.* (2005). These scholars contend that disparities and existing societal inequalities can serve as major motivators for individuals to engage in self-employment and entrepreneurial activities. They elaborate on this by highlighting the diligence and perseverance exhibited by individuals from disadvantaged backgrounds in finding innovative solutions, empowering them to achieve success in entrepreneurship, as emphasized by Packard and Bylund (2018). Additionally, they argue that in the long term, entrepreneurship, as a driver of economic prosperity and well-being, can help reduce inequality (Packard and Bylund, 2018).

The same debate extended to the relation between inequality and international entrepreneurship. While inequality can act as a hindrance to entrepreneurs expanding their activities to the global markets, it can be true that inequality is a fostering factor. To elaborate, inequality, as a widely known phenomenon, creates an uneven playing field for entrepreneurs, hindering their ability to compete effectively on the international stage. These entrepreneurs face various problems including limited access to crucial resources, and in terms of some of developing countries, restricted access to global markets due to sanctions (Luo and Bu, 2016). These terms can incentivize entrepreneurs to change their target and adopt a different strategy: internationalization (Jafari-Sadeghi *et al.*, 2020b). Additionally, when we limit the level of analysis to an entrepreneur, it can be stated that the high level of uncertainty may not be tolerated. In this regard, they seek to find another solution which is less risky and less uncertain. When these business people find the cross-border activities less hostile, less uncertain, and more propitious, they may come to decide to expand their activities to the international market.

However, it can also be stated that lack of access to needed-resources, having problems in establishing reliable and acceptable connection with businesses, and uncertainty prevalent in the socio-economic structure of a country could hamper their endeavor toward internationalization. Hence, this showcases a problem. Since institutional factors can be cumbersome enough to pull entrepreneurs back, the sense of inequality can exacerbate their moving forward. Previous studies such as Pindado *et al.* (2023) stated that for making international decisions, institutional factors play an important role. This means that the regulations, rules, and legal frameworks have a direct effect on the internationalization decisions of entrepreneurs. This statement aligns with Peng's (2003) theory of institutional voids. He propounded that the lack of institutions can negatively impact businesses. This demonstrates that the internal factors of a country are of great significance for entrepreneurs (Sciascia *et al.*, 2012). In this regard, in the following paragraphs, we intend to make the relationship between a country's institutions and internationalization a little clearer.

5.2 Institutions and Internationalization

Peng's (2003) theory of institutional voids posits that weak or absent formal institutions in developing economies create a significant handicap for businesses operating inside their borders. These institutions, encompassing legal frameworks, regulatory bodies, and enforcement mechanisms, provide a crucial foundation for smooth market functioning and business development. Their absence or inadequacy creates an environment of uncertainty and inefficiency, further compounding the challenges faced by entrepreneurial firms. This institutional void contributes to a persistent global inequality in the business landscape, where firms from developed economies benefit from a more robust and supportive institutional environment. In this regard, while from a narrower perspective, internal institutions can be an important factor for internationalization, the institutions in the host country are important as well. The reason for this is when entrepreneurs aim at internationalization, they have to address the specific items related to the host country. For instance, they need to consider what are the legally-restricted actions and behaviors for foreign companies. Also, they need to know how specific terms can be enacted to ensure the safety of their products and their business. Therefore, noticing the institutional consideration related to the host country is of great significance for entrepreneurs aiming at internationalization.

From the internal perspective, institutional void or weakness can suitably be propitious for internationalization. The concept of institutional escapism, as stated by Pindado *et al.* (2023), posits that limitations imposed by the domestic environment, such as restricted access to financing or complex regulations, can incentivize firms to seek a more favorable environment abroad. Also, the stage of internationalization and the venture's resources play a crucial role. In this regard, while some rules and regulations can be favorable or neutral for some firms, other firms may find it harmful due to their resource conditions to answer proportionately to the institutional factors. Therefore, for some firms, internationalization becomes a strategic response – a calculated move to circumvent domestic limitations and ensure the viability and growth of their business. By venturing into international markets, entrepreneurial firms can gain access to a wider array of resources, expand their networks, and enhance their operational efficiency and effectiveness (Pindado *et al.*, 2023). Also, by adopting an escapism strategy, ventures manage the uncertainty in their home country environment and attempt to stabilize their venture in a less hostile and turbulent atmosphere where their ventures face less uncertainty and unpredictable changes. This issue becomes more concerning when we address it in the context of developing countries.

Moreover, the institutional forces may compel ventures to stay in their home country and restrict their presence in the international environment. This situation, which is called institution constraint, hinders a business's attempts to become involved in international interactions (Pindado *et al.*, 2023). This institutional constraint can be observed in many of the ventures operating in developing countries.

However, from the perspective of opportunity, developing countries have a greater potential for entrepreneurship. To be more specific, the strategic advantages of internationalization for entrepreneurial firms in developing economies extend beyond mere market access. Research by Luo and Bu (2018a) highlights several specific strengths that these firms possess, which translate well to the international arena. One such advantage is their greater propensity for ambidexterity. This refers to the ability to simultaneously balance exploration, the pursuit of new opportunities and innovative ventures, with exploitation, the optimization of existing resources and processes. This agility allows them to adapt to the dynamic and ever-changing nature of international markets. Additionally, these firms often have established networks within their home countries, fostering valuable business relationships and facilitating knowledge transfer (Luo and Bu, 2016). These networks can act as springboards for international expansion, providing access to local partners and market knowledge in target countries. Furthermore,

5.2. Institutions and Internationalization

regarding the uncertain and agitated nature of many developing countries, entrepreneurial firms often demonstrate superiority in achieving survivability and adaptability in challenging and turbulent environments (Luo and Bu, 2016). This resilience stems from their experience navigating the complexities and uncertainties of their own domestic markets. In this regard, these firms have less problems in operating with limited resources; thus, they are more potent to overcome bureaucratic hurdles, which equips them well for the challenges of navigating diverse international markets. Therefore, it can be stated that institutional factors can play a positive or negative role in their relations with internationalization.

Furthermore, previous studies have mentioned the specific barriers that the gender of an entrepreneur places on them in the process of choosing escapism or constraint strategies (Pindado *et al.*, 2023). These studies stated that in many countries, the situation for women entrepreneurs is harder. To elaborate, women in many societies have to comply with specific norms and expectations. These expectations restrict them to behave in a specific way and be involved in specific fields. Owing to the fact that these beliefs directly and indirectly affect the strategy they opt for and the support they receive from their families, society, and investors, it is harder for them to be involved in these strategies.

In order to make internationalization easier for entrepreneurial firms, previous studies such as Jafari-Sadeghi *et al.* (2022) have stated that the impact of facilitating tools such as digital technology can be of great significance. This importance can be attributed to the dominance of digital technology in almost all fields and the fact this factor has been considered as a transformative force. In this regard, in the following paragraphs, we intend to elucidate the degree to which digital technology can play a part in the internationalization of entrepreneurial ventures and their strive to adopt or circumvent the institutional barriers.

5.3 Digital Technology as a Tool for Fostering International Entrepreneurship

The emergence of digital technology, characterized as a phenomenon rooted in knowledge dissemination and mobility, has brought about profound changes across various fields of science and expertise, as evidenced by studies conducted by Huang *et al.* (2024), Ongo Nkoa and Song (2023), and Rahman *et al.* (2023). This technological revolution encompasses a wide array of tools such as social media, the Internet of Things (IoT), Artificial Intelligence, and 3D printers, which have not only reshaped market dynamics and social frameworks on a global scale but have also created new avenues for entrepreneurial endeavors, as highlighted by Gregori and Holzmann (2020), and Rippa and Secundo (2019). According to Nambisan (2017), digital technology serves as a transformative and disruptive force that challenges traditional linear business models, ushering in a more flexible and unpredictable approach to conducting business operations.

Numerous scholarly works have regarded digital technology as a force for equilibrium and empowerment, positing it as a tool that can empower underprivileged populations and individuals in developing nations to bridge the gap with their more advantaged counterparts in developed countries, a notion supported by Dy *et al.* (2017), Kelly and McAdam (2022), and Nambisan (2017). Entrepreneurs worldwide, particularly those hailing from developing nations, leverage digital tools to not only overcome business obstacles and innovate but also enhance the efficiency and efficacy of their enterprises, as observed in the works of Dana *et al.* (2022a,b), Ongo Nkoa and Song (2023), and Rippa and Secundo (2019).

The integration of digital technology offers entrepreneurial entities across the globe a more equitable playing field, with digital platforms playing a pivotal role in empowering marginalized entrepreneurs and addressing challenging issues of inequality. For example, crowdfunding platforms serve as a vital link connecting newly internationalized firms grappling with financial limitations to potential investors worldwide, thereby furnishing them with essential resources and financial backing, a phenomenon explored by Cumming *et al.* (2024), Huo *et al.* (2024),

5.3. Digital Technology as a Tool

and Ratten (2023). Moreover, these platforms enhance the visibility and credibility of these emerging internationalized firms, aiding them in navigating the complexities associated with operating in foreign markets, as discussed by Kang (2022), and Kelly and McAdam (2022).

In the context of this study, it can be stated that digital revolution has fundamentally reshaped the landscape of international entrepreneurship. This technology, by dismantling geographical barriers and democratizing access to resources, empowers entrepreneurs across the globe to extend their operations beyond their boundaries and navigate the complexities of international markets.

Traditionally, ventures aimed at international operation faced various obstacles such as significant entry barriers, including high overhead costs, complex logistics, and limited market reach. For instance, e-commerce platforms like Shopify and Amazon Marketplace eliminate the need for physical storefronts, allowing international businesses to access global markets with minimal investment. Additionally, social media marketing and search engine optimization (SEO) techniques enable international entrepreneurs to target specific customer segments across borders, bypassing geographical limitations and promoting their products or services directly to a global audience. Hence, businesses can improve their efficiency and access their targeted customers in an optimum way. Furthermore, the Internet has made network establishment and extension an easy task for entrepreneurs. Previously, entrepreneurs had no choice but to spend a great deal of their business's resources to establish their necessary relationships with their peers around the globe. However, with the introduction of the Internet, these obstacles and hardships have finished and made network building a common task among entrepreneurs in an international environment (Glavas and Mathews, 2014).

Digital tools also set the stage for international collaboration and networking opportunities for entrepreneurs around the globe. Online platforms like Upwork and Fiverr connect businesses with skilled professionals worldwide, facilitating the formation of geographically dispersed teams with diverse skillsets. This makes working for both businesses and employees easier. This way of running a business, by utilizing digital technology, also helps both sides, business owners and employees, to have bargaining power and gain the ability to reach more desirable employees and positions. Similarly, social media platforms like LinkedIn create virtual communities for entrepreneurs to connect with international partners, mentors, and investors, fostering knowledge sharing, resource exchange, and potential business collaborations. These digital tools not only facilitate the international presence of entrepreneurs, but also assist women around the globe to shun the stereotypes prevalent in their societies and work toward materializing their passion for entrepreneurship (Pindado *et al.*, 2023).

Moreover, owing to the fact that securing essential resources has been a problem for businesses, digital platforms helped them to manage and surmount this obstacle. To be more specific, there are various platforms that connect businesses to potential investors around the globe. Once an arduous problem, thanks to digital platforms this problem has become a thing of the past. For instance, digital platforms like Kickstarter and Indiegogo have revolutionized access to capital for international entrepreneurs. These platforms assist businesses to bypass traditional financial institutions and raise capital directly from a global audience and investors. This empowers entrepreneurs from around the globe, particularly in developing countries where access to traditional funding may be limited, to compete on a more level playing field. These crowdfunding platforms also serve as valuable market validation tools, allowing entrepreneurs to assess international interest about their idea before significant investment.

6

Contextual Factors in IE

Context stands out as one of the most crucial elements, if not the absolute paramount factor, that molds the intention of an entrepreneur to internationalize their endeavors. The context, encompassing social, cultural, and economic dimensions, holds the power to directly influence an individual's engagement in entrepreneurial activities. At the individual level, context becomes intricately intertwined with the dynamics of how people within a specific country or region interact amongst themselves and the prevailing beliefs that shape their societal norms. This implies that although individuals possess a certain degree of autonomy and decision-making authority, contextual elements wield a significant impact on their choices. Particularly, social and cultural norms play a pivotal role in the decision-making process. Cultural factors, in particular, can act as potent catalysts or deterrents. While certain cultural beliefs may serve as powerful drivers, fostering an entrepreneurial spirit, globally pervasive attitudes can pose obstacles. One prevailing example lies in the perception of women. Across various nations, a prevailing notion persists that women hold an inferior status compared to men and are deemed incapable of undertaking strenuous or complex tasks. These entrenched beliefs hold immense significance as they not only influence an entrepreneur's self-belief and determination but also sway the perceptions of potential investors regarding their capabilities (Bachmann et al., 2024), thus impacting the legitimacy of their business ventures. To delve deeper into this pressing matter, the subsequent paragraphs aim to delve into the role of women in entrepreneurship and its intersection with established theories and existing literature on international business.

6.1 Women in Entrepreneurship

Gender has been a topic of scholarly discourse across various scientific disciplines, including psychology, sociology, and economics (Boggio et al., 2020). Prior studies demonstrated that there is a significant difference between gender and sex. there are studies that utilized these terms interchangeably. Moreover, some studies stated that recognizing this difference is a promising step toward understanding this notion that many differences between women and men are societal rather than natural. Therefore, in this study, we follow the same path as prominent researchers (e.g., Cowden et al., 2023; Gupta et al., 2009) have undertaken and maintain that gender is a socially constructed concept, whereas sex pertains to biological characteristics.

Within the realm of entrepreneurship, gender has been an attractive and, simultaneously, a controversial topic among scholars. Researchers propounded that by taking the social congruity role theory (SCRT) into account- which states that each gender behaves in a way that aligns with cultural and social expectations of their environment- individuals prefer to comply with the cultural and social norms in order to avoid any unfavorable consequences such as social sanctions and negative evaluations.

There are studies (e.g., Anglin et al., 2018; Bendell et al., 2020; Yang et al., 2020a,b) that assert entrepreneurship is not only gendered but also masculine. These studies contend that there are stereotypes associated with entrepreneurs (e.g., aggressiveness, autonomy, competitiveness, innovation, determination, and risk-taking) that are more proximate to masculinity than femininity (Anglin et al., 2018). These studies also pointed out that owing to the women's greater risk-aversion, which could account for their lower loss acceptability, their willingness to evaluate opportunities (Shinnar et al., 2012), and could work against the flexibility element of effectuation, and their predilection to preclude themselves from entrepreneurial activities (Bendell et al., 2020), men are expected to be better entrepreneurs.

Conversely, there are studies (e.g., Hassan and Ayub, 2019) that adhere to the notion that women possess higher levels of emotional intelligence and are capable of outperforming men in the field of entrepreneurship (Cowden et al., 2023). These studies claim that women are not only better entrepreneurs but they are also better effectuators. They believe that when it comes to employing effectuation, as a logic of decision-making, women entrepreneurs are more effective given the characteristics that are believed to be more aligned with that of women such as co-creation, mean-orientation, and the ability to cope with uncertainty. These traits demand sundry features (e.g., kindness, sharing of resources, trustfulness, and network extension) that are more commonly attributed to women than men (Cowden et al., 2023).

Considering the point that these beliefs regarding a specific part of a society, here women, can seriously impact the attitude and mainstream belief regarding women, it is demanding to address a concerning issue: their legitimacy. Since legitimacy in a society of people or business firms denotes the specific way that a firm or an entrepreneur in perceived and evaluated, it is necessary to understand how this element can affect the prosperity of women-led businesses and motivate them to venture into new markets. In this regard, in the following paragraphs, we will discuss legitimacy in women's entrepreneurship.

6.2   Women Entrepreneurs and Legitimacy

Entrepreneurship, as a phenomenon, does not exist in a vacuum but rather thrives within an interactive environment where initial assessments of an entrepreneur or their venture are influenced by the prevailing circumstances and surroundings (Prochotta et al., 2022). The impact of these evaluations on how individuals are perceived by others necessitates a thorough examination of entrepreneurial behaviors in order to achieve success and prosperity (Rutherford and Nagy, 2014). The evaluation of entrepreneurs by their communities and environments plays a crucial role in shaping the perception of "desirability and appropriateness within the social framework of norms, values, and beliefs" (Oware et al., 2022; Suchman, 1995), a concept known as legitimacy. It is imperative for individuals to garner positive assessments in their interactions with others as these evaluations directly influence their responses and opportunities (Zamantılı Nayır and Shinnar, 2020). In the realm of entrepreneurship, evaluators must deem an entrepreneurial endeavor as desirable, suitable, and capable of eliciting actions such as attracting financial investments to confer legitimacy (Liu et al., 2019; Rutherford and Nagy, 2014), which in turn facilitates the acquisition of essential resources and enhances access to resources like capital and skilled personnel (Kašperová, 2021; Stenholm and Hytti, 2014; Vershinina et al., 2020). The availability of resources is pivotal for the survival and sustainability of a nascent venture, particularly during its initial phases (Javadian et al., 2021).

The evaluation of entrepreneurs within their social and cultural contexts underscores the significant impact of institutional factors, such as culture and societal norms, on these assessments (Stenholm and Hytti, 2014). Specifically, cultural beliefs and societal norms exert influence on the growth and legitimacy of a firm or a new venture (Kašperová, 2021; Vershinina et al., 2020). Within this framework, stereotypes, including gender stereotypes, serve as socio-cultural elements prevalent in societies that reflect societal evaluations (Prochotta et al., 2022). These stereotypes, particularly gender stereotypes, result in individuals receiving positive reinforcement only when they conform to widely-accepted norms, including gender role expectations. Consequently, women, who are often associated with traits like kindness, compassion, communalism, and risk aversion rather than aggressiveness, competitiveness, and risk-taking (Bendell et al., 2020; Javadian et al., 2021), are often perceived to have lower involvement in entrepreneurial pursuits (Liu et al., 2019). Previous research has characterized entrepreneurship as not only gendered but also masculine (Gupta et al., 2009, 2014). In alignment with societal and cultural beliefs, studies have revealed that businesses owned by women tend to be smaller in scale, less oriented towards growth, and less profitable compared to those owned by men, often operating in sectors where little value is added (Vershinina *et al.*, 2020). This showcases the inferiority of femininity to masculinity. In this situation, women entrepreneurs as the representative of underrepresented portion of almost all societies have two choices. They may succumb to disappointment and forgo entrepreneurship due to the highly difficult of its nature, or avert their business focus from internal to external markets and thus involve in internationalization (Jafari-Sadeghi *et al.*, 2020a).

In this regard, there are studies that demonstrated that these under-representative portions of the society that are dealing with many arduous problems in the process of establishing their own entrepreneurial ventures inside or outside of the country can leverage various tools to materialize their intention. One these well-known tools is digital technology. According to prior studies, digital technology has a potential to not only empower them survive in the unpalatable situation of their country and reach survival but also can go further and contribute to the sustainability. Considering its important contribution, we elaborate on it in the following paragraphs.

6.3 Digital Technology: A Levelling Tool for Entrepreneurs

The era of digital transformation, characterized by the emergence of social media, the Internet of Things (IoT), Artificial Intelligence, and 3D printing (Huang *et al.*, 2024), has fundamentally altered global markets and social frameworks. This revolution has inaugurated a fresh phase for business visionaries, presenting them with a plethora of prospects (Gregori and Holzmann, 2020). Nambisan (2017) posits that digital technologies act as disruptive influences, deconstructing traditional linear business models and nurturing a more vibrant and uncertain entrepreneurial environment.

The theory of social inclusion proposes that digital technologies possess the capability to act as a potent equalizer. By granting access to innovative tools to marginalized groups, such as women, these technologies can assist in bridging the divide between them and more established entities Dy *et al.* (2017). Entrepreneurs can utilize these tools to surmount obstacles, foster innovation, and enhance operational efficiency

(Holzmann and Gregori, 2023). Nambisan (2017) outlines three fundamental elements of digital technology pertinent to entrepreneurship: digital artifacts, digital platforms, and digital infrastructures.

Digital artifacts, as elucidated by Kelly and McAdam (2022), represent independent applications or media content. Digital platforms, according to Nambisan (2017), furnish a communal framework that accommodates complementary offerings, encompassing digital artifacts. These platforms empower female entrepreneurs by easing their entry into new markets, broadening their range of products and services, generating customer value, and attaining a competitive advantage (Nambisan, 2017). Lastly, digital infrastructure, as expounded by Kelly and McAdam (2022), pertains to the technological tools and systems that facilitate collaboration, communication, and computation.

For aspiring and female entrepreneurs seeking to engage in the global arena, digital technologies present a myriad of advantages. These resources can aid in expanding their professional connections, enriching their knowledge base, overcoming resource constraints, boosting productivity, and accessing novel prospects (Bachmann *et al.*, 2024). Consequently, this could result in heightened self-assurance and belief in oneself, ultimately leading to a greater propensity for these entrepreneurs to partake in and pursue entrepreneurial ventures (Rahman *et al.*, 2023). Hence, digital technology serves as an equalizing instrument for these entrepreneurs to participate more actively in entrepreneurship and fortify their international presence.

The influence of the involvement of these entrepreneurs in the global arena transcends individual implications, with substantial repercussions at the national level. Research by Khoo *et al.* (2023), Kamberidou (2020), and Ongo Nkoa and Song (2023) accentuates the possible advantages for governments, including the creation of employment opportunities, economic advancement, and alleviation of poverty. However, Khoo *et al.* (2023) present a disquieting statistic: only 13 developed nations have enacted policies explicitly supporting women's utilization of digital technologies in their entrepreneurial undertakings. This underscores the necessity for a broader shift towards policies that empower women to harness the full potential of digital technologies in their entrepreneurial pursuits.

6.4 Moving Beyond Survival and Toward Sustainability

Digital technology (DT) has emerged as a liberating and empowering tool for marginalized groups within the realm of entrepreneurship, such as those located in developing nations (Kelly and McAdam, 2022; Salamzadeh *et al.*, 2024). The utilization of these digital tools presents a multitude of opportunities for entrepreneurs. Initially, they can utilize DT to overcome the negative impacts of various challenges, including gender biases that are prevalent in the entrepreneurial landscape, especially for women entrepreneurs, and subsequently develop innovative and sustainable solutions for the obstacles they encounter in their business operations (Sharma *et al.*, 2023). To delve deeper, there exist numerous contextual barriers that impede the advancement of entrepreneurs, such as societal gender norms that hinder women from establishing their own ventures (Javadian *et al.*, 2021). Within the entrepreneurial sphere, a plethora of issues such as difficulties in accessing essential resources, established distribution networks, and appropriate education obstruct entrepreneurs, especially those who are new to the field and women, from achieving success in their ventures. Consequently, as per prior research findings (e.g., Javadian *et al.*, 2021; Vershinina *et al.*, 2020), these entrepreneurs are often associated with smaller, less profitable businesses that cater to narrower market segments. Nonetheless, DT has provided them with the means to effectively and efficiently navigate through these challenges (Kelly and McAdam, 2022). Furthermore, digital technology is not merely aiding in the survival of businesses; it is propelling them towards sustainability. With this in mind, the subsequent paragraphs elaborate on the specific ways in which digital technology can enhance the sustainability considerations of a business.

6.5 Entrepreneurs and Benefits of Utilizing Digital Technology: Environmental Sustainability

Research conducted by Salamzadeh *et al.* (2022) has highlighted a strong correlation between digital technologies and environmental sustainability. The incorporation of these technologies has the potential to significantly improve sustainability by enabling eco-friendly production processes and models. This is particularly achievable through the utilization of artificial intelligence and the combined capabilities of various digital tools, as mentioned by Broccardo *et al.* (2023). Further exploration reveals that digital technology possesses the capability to establish environmentally conscious businesses by embedding sustainability deep within an organization's core identity and operations. This surpasses traditional optimization methods and results in the creation of value that encompasses ecological, economic, and technological aspects, as articulated by Szabó *et al.* (2023). Additionally, it introduces groundbreaking opportunities for environmental monitoring, protection, and the advancement of global sustainability, as pointed out by Rosário and Dias (2022). Moreover, the utilization of digital technologies in sustainable business models can streamline the generation, delivery, and capture of value, despite the challenges in implementation highlighted by Cricelli and Strazzullo (2021).

However, it is crucial to acknowledge that digital technologies also have environmental downsides. The processing of data and the generation of electronic waste contribute to the release of harmful carbon emissions, as emphasized by Wang *et al.* (2022). This underscores the importance of having a comprehensive understanding of environmental sustainability within the digital domain, going beyond just carbon reduction, according to Szabó *et al.* (2023). To elaborate further, the integration of digital technology in businesses can lead to various environmental challenges, including electronic waste accumulation, increased energy consumption, elevated carbon emissions, disparities in access (digital divide), job instability, the rise of monopolies, and concerns related to data security, as elucidated by Dean and McMullen (2007).

Nonetheless, despite the differing opinions on the connection between digitalization and environmental sustainability, these technologies offer significant advantages for emerging and disadvantaged entrepreneurs striving to promote a sustainable and eco-friendly future, as proposed by Salamzadeh *et al.* (2022). For instance, female entrepreneurs, due to their inherent eco-conscious tendencies, can utilize digital technologies to develop sustainable products, explore renewable energy sources, and engage in environmentally friendly innovations, as highlighted by Zelezny *et al.* (2000). Furthermore, businesses led by women are more likely to integrate sustainability into their operational models and policies, creating a positive feedback loop. By prioritizing sustainability, these female-led enterprises can build a strong reputation and increased credibility among their customers and stakeholders, as discussed by Dana *et al.* (2022b) and Frydrych *et al.* (2014).

6.6 Entrepreneurs and Benefits of Utilizing Digital Technology: Economic Sustainability

The correlation between economic sustainability and digital technologies is intricate and diverse. Digital technologies present a myriad of opportunities for organizations to embrace sustainable business practices and create sustainable products, including but not limited to renewable energy solutions, smart cities, and tools for sustainable consumption, as highlighted by Rosário and Dias (2022). Both startups and well-established companies are actively exploring digital sustainable business models that fuse environmental and economic factors, ultimately resulting in favorable outcomes, as noted by Böttcher *et al.* (2024).

Nevertheless, the adoption and integration of digital technologies into sustainable business models present various challenges. These obstacles encompass constraints in effectively harnessing these technologies for sustainability objectives, as identified by Fuerst *et al.* (2023). Research studies, for instance, those conducted by Broccardo *et al.* (2023) and Chopra *et al.* (2024), underscore the significance of infusing sustainability into strategies supported by digital technologies. This amalgamation not only enhances performance and profitability but also underscores the robust interconnection between digitalization, sustainability, and financial success. Conversely, effectively addressing challenges like e-waste management, energy consumption, and data security is imperative to fully capitalize on the potential of digital technologies for economic sustainability, as highlighted by Sun *et al.* (2020) and Wang *et al.* (2022).

In order to attain ecological and economic sustainability, companies, regardless of their size or tenure, must embark on two critical transformations concurrently: digital transformation and sustainable business model evolution, as emphasized by Böttcher *et al.* (2024). Within this context, digital technologies play a pivotal role in enhancing the effectiveness, efficiency, and profitability of both individuals and organizations, thereby contributing to economic sustainability, as articulated by Chopra *et al.* (2024).

6.7 Entrepreneurs and Benefits of Utilizing Digital Technology: Social Sustainability

Digital technologies are of paramount significance in the advancement of social sustainability through the enhancement of connectivity, communication, as well as the accessibility to information, as highlighted by Rosário and Dias (2022). The incorporation of digital technology across various sectors has the potential to bring about enhanced social outcomes, including but not limited to heightened availability of educational resources, healthcare services, and employment prospects, hence making a notable contribution to the realm of social sustainability, as expounded by Xiao and Su (2022). Through the more proficient utilization of digital technologies, societies are better equipped to effectively tackle social obstacles, foster inclusivity, empower both individuals and communities to engage in decision-making procedures, and ultimately nurture social sustainability, as pointed out by Khan *et al.* (2021). It is widely acknowledged that digital technologies play a pivotal role in promoting social inclusivity, amplifying connectivity, and facilitating a broader integration of various stakeholders, as emphasized by Fuerst *et al.* (2023).

7

Emerging Themes

International entrepreneurship has emerged as a dynamic and extensive field of academic study, reflecting the complexities and dynamics of global business activities. This section explores several key and emerging issues at the core of international entrepreneurship, particularly the internationalization of small and medium-sized enterprises (SMEs), the rise of global startups, and the acceleration of digital entrepreneurship. These topics shape current research and point toward future research questions and practices.

The internationalization process is both a crucial endeavor and a significant challenge for SMEs transitioning from local markets to international arenas. This transition accompanies limited resources, a lack of market-specific knowledge, and legal complexities. However, these companies often leverage their inherent flexibility and innovation to establish significant positions in foreign markets. The rise of digital technologies and e-commerce platforms has also enabled SMEs to reach global audiences effectively at relatively lower costs. Alongside the internationalization of SMEs is the phenomenon of global startups. Compared to traditional companies that gradually expand globally, they start with a worldwide perspective and use innovative technologies and business models to accelerate their international growth. The founders of these startups often have global experience and networks, helping them manage the complexities of multiple markets simultaneously. In digital entrepreneurship, the Internet and mobile technologies have revolutionized how companies operate and access international markets. This transformation has had the most significant impact through the emergence of digital platforms serving global audiences, democratizing access to international markets, and lowering entry barriers. Digital entrepreneurship includes e-commerce, fintech innovations, digital marketing, and the gig economy, collectively contributing to a more connected and dynamic global economy.

Overall, these themes indicate a larger shift towards more globally integrated and socially conscious business practices. Thus, the field of international entrepreneurship not only provides insights into the expansion of business across borders but also reflects broader socio-economic trends influencing global business strategies. Future research in this area is likely to delve deeper into these topics, uncovering new insights and providing guidance for entrepreneurs and policymakers in navigating the increasingly complex landscape of international trade.

7.1 Internationalization of Small and Medium Enterprises (SMEs)

The internationalization of small and medium-sized enterprises (SMEs) in recent decades has become a significant and crucial topic in academia and scientific research, addressing the challenges and opportunities of this process at a global level. Internationalization of SMEs refers to the expansion of activities and entry into global markets, which can significantly enhance the performance and competitiveness of these companies. Research indicates that numerous factors influence the internationalization process of SMEs, including the optimal use of financial resources, the utilization of information technology (IT) as a primary tool for accessing global markets, the creation of effective networks with other companies and distribution channels, communication capabilities and international cooperation, reduction of transaction costs, and leveraging human resources with international expertise. In this context, improving

7.1. Internationalization of Small and Medium Enterprises (SMEs)

financial strategies and employing new technologies to enhance performance, strengthening communication networks, developing global markets, and efficient management of human resources are effective measures for the internationalization of SMEs. Moreover, focusing on the internal capabilities and resources of companies as a fundamental factor in international development and enhancing their competitiveness is highly significant. Summarizing these points, it can be concluded that the international development of SMEs not only increases access to global markets but also helps improve the performance and added value of these companies, thus warranting special attention to this matter (Anwar et al., 2023; Fernandes et al., 2023).

Researchers have examined emerging trends in the internationalization of SMEs, employing modern techniques such as machine learning and reference management systems to identify topics like resource-based theory, dynamic capabilities, international entrepreneurship, and duality for further research. These approaches suggest that the use of advanced technologies and data science can aid in analyzing and predicting complex trends in the internationalization of SMEs, thereby gaining a deeper understanding of this process. These areas have been proposed as promising topics for further research and present opportunities for significant advancements in improving SMEs' internationalization strategies and policies (Flores, 2022).

Furthermore, recent research has investigated the impact of internalization, globalization, and artificial intelligence on the global landscape of SMEs. These studies show that these fundamental factors not only contribute to the development and expansion of international activities of SMEs but also emphasize the importance of effective management of export operations and the creation of appropriate strategies to enhance growth and profitability in global markets. Internalization, as a process focused on internal improvement and strengthening of companies and their internal communications, can facilitate internationalization processes and provide the necessary capabilities to enter global markets. Globalization, as a process of acquiring entry and international presence, plays a crucial role in increasing access to new markets and expanding foreign activities. Additionally, artificial intelligence, as an innovative technology, offers companies the ability to evaluate complex data, predict trends, and improve decision-making processes in international environments. The application of artificial intelligence in managing export operations can help improve strategic decision-making, enhance operational efficiency, and reduce transaction costs (Johansson and Persson, 2018; Wei and Pardo, 2022).

7.2 The Strategy of Small and Medium-Sized Enterprises (SMEs) in Connecting to Global Markets

Small and medium-sized enterprises (SMEs) can pursue various pathways for internationalization. Studies on manufacturing SMEs in New Zealand have identified two primary pathways to internationalization: one with a focus on global scope and the other on regional concentration. In the global scope pathway, companies strive to enter global markets by expanding their products and services. These companies often employ international market expansion strategies, such as entering new markets, increasing production capacity, and utilizing international distribution networks. Production locations are also strategically selected to optimize costs and enhance access to diverse markets. Conversely, in the regional concentration pathway, companies focus more on strengthening their presence and activities in regional or sometimes national markets. They typically employ strategies such as offering more localized services and developing close relationships with customers and suppliers. This strategy enables them to compete more effectively by providing services and products tailored to regional needs and improving relationships with customers and suppliers. Overall, the strategic configuration in these two pathways, including product and market selection, market development approach, and production location, is crucial. Each of these strategies helps companies successfully advance in their internationalization process and achieve their international goals (Chetty and Campbell-Hunt, 2003).

When examining emerging markets, SMEs face unique approaches to internationalization. Compared to larger companies, SMEs encounter specific challenges such as a lack of financial resources, limited access to information, and insufficient workforce. To overcome these obstacles, they employ creative strategies that help them successfully enter global markets. For example, they can leverage local knowledge and communication networks better to understand the trends and needs of their target markets and optimize their resources. In addressing obstacles such as capital shortages, information gaps, and a lack of skilled personnel, SMEs can focus on using innovative economic and technological solutions. Careful planning in choosing target markets, providing quality products and services, and using digital solutions for communication and marketing are effective strategies that help these companies improve their competitiveness on an international scale. As a result, with appropriate strategic approaches, SMEs can effectively participate in global markets and benefit from international opportunities (Khambhata, 2023; Weiermair and Peters, 1998).

The internationalization of SMEs is generally a dynamic and evolutionary process that changes over time and is heavily influenced by the internal characteristics of the firm and shifting market conditions. This process encompasses several stages in which companies must adapt to new environments and optimize their strategies to maximize existing opportunities. Characteristics such as industry type, company size, management's international knowledge and experience, and access to financial and human resources play significant roles in determining the pace and manner of internationalization. Additionally, market conditions are a critical factor in the internationalization process. Trade barriers, the level of competition in target markets, and changes in the economic and trade policies of countries can profoundly impact the international strategies of companies. Therefore, SMEs must continuously analyze their business environments and respond to new market opportunities to succeed globally. This flexibility and ability to adapt to changes are key to success in internationalization (Kamakura *et al.*, 2012).

7.3 Global Startups

Global startups and international entrepreneurs are pivotal in the world of international business and significantly contribute to its shaping and evolution. Research in this area underscores the importance of entrepreneurs adopting a global mindset. Such a perspective enables them not only to recognize opportunities beyond their geographical boundaries but also to address international developments and challenges more effectively. A global mindset allows entrepreneurs to introduce their innovations to new markets and leverage knowledge and technologies from around the world. This can significantly enhance the international performance of small companies and startups, aiding them in confidently penetrating global markets and improving their international competitiveness. Moreover, a global mindset helps entrepreneurs better understand the diverse cultures and needs of global markets, allowing them to adapt their marketing and sales strategies flexibly to accommodate these differences. Entrepreneurs with a global mindset are more adept at identifying and exploiting international opportunities and can navigate the complexities and dynamics of global markets more efficiently. These skills and perspectives lay the foundation for long-term success in the international arena, strengthening the sustainability and growth of businesses (Becker-Ritterspach *et al.*, 2017; Hisrich, 2015; Chowdhury and Audretsch, 2021).

Beyond the previously discussed aspects, the concept of Born Global companies is also noteworthy. These companies aim for global markets right from their inception, foregoing traditional methods of internationalization. Unlike traditional models that follow gradual steps to enter international markets, Born Global companies begin with a global vision and rapidly seek to expand operations and sales internationally. This strategy enables them to overcome geographical limitations and achieve high productivity from global opportunities. Growth centers play a crucial role in supporting these Born Global companies. These centers, known as incubators, provide essential resources, advice, access to business and specialist networks, and other critical services to help startups quickly grow in global markets. This support includes assistance in technology, management, market strategies, and even financing, which are necessary to accelerate the internationalization process. With the effective support of these centers, Born Global companies can manage the challenges of entering new markets and consolidate their competitive positions in the global arena (Maciejewski and Wach, 2019; Cavusgil and Knight, 2015).

It is crucial to note that an entrepreneur's desire and ability to internationalize, even before establishing a startup, significantly influence the future direction and success of the startup's international activities. These attributes reflect the international mindset that an entrepreneur possesses during the early stages of business development. Entrepreneurs with a global perspective often seek opportunities beyond their domestic market and aim to establish international networks and connections from the start. This mindset leads entrepreneurs to design their strategies and business plans according to global market standards and conditions from the outset. They not only customize their products or services for different markets but also consider the various cultures, laws, and needs of international consumers. This approach results in the development of strategies designed for global success from the beginning, enabling entrepreneurs to enter international markets more quickly and exploit new opportunities promptly. Such strategic thinking not only supports the survival and growth of businesses in dynamic global environments but also fosters the creation of sustainable competitive advantages in the international arena (Costa *et al.*, 2023).

In examining emerging economies, development strategies often emphasize the crucial role of domestic companies, especially high-tech startups, in establishing connections and cooperative links with global markets. This strategic approach assists companies in accelerating their growth and development through access to larger markets and new opportunities. A direct presence in global markets not only enhances knowledge and access to new resources but also provides opportunities to transfer technical knowledge and gain international competitive advantages. This strategy is particularly feasible for startups in technology fields because technology facilitates faster and more efficient communication, which is vital in the global arena. Additionally, developing cooperative links with other companies and organizations worldwide can improve technological innovation and effectiveness, reducing barriers to business development. This approach not only fosters the growth of startups but also plays a key role in achieving the long-term development goals of emerging economies. By strengthening the private sector and encouraging entrepreneurship, it lays the foundation for economic and social progress at both national and international levels (Cieślik and Cieślik, 2017).

7.4 Networking for Global Startups and International Entrepreneurs

Networking for global startups and international entrepreneurs is one of the most critical aspects of success in the global arena. This activity not only plays a role in the transfer of knowledge and information between entrepreneurs and companies, but also serves as a platform for searching for partnership opportunities and strategic collaborations. Networking provides opportunities to exchange experiences, resources, technologies, and innovative ideas that can help accelerate the growth and development of startups. On the other hand, networking in the business world allows entrepreneurs to gain access to new markets and get to know different cultures and market structures. These interactions can lead to the discovery of business partnerships and joint ventures where both parties benefit from each other's expertise and resources. In addition, networking provides opportunities to learn and improve skills through workshops, seminars, and networking events organized by business and industry associations, all of which help strengthen the overall capabilities of entrepreneurs on a global scale. As a result, networking not only helps to improve the skills and knowledge of entrepreneurs but also enables them to continue their international activities with more confidence and a better understanding of the challenges and opportunities at the global level (Ramírez and Levy, 2022).

Recent studies have emphasized the importance of networking activities in international business contexts and have shown how these activities can help increase the performance of international new ventures (InVS). Knowledge sharing is among the main benefits of networking, as it allows network members to share their experiences, information, and technologies. This improves decision-making and reduces risks in challenging business environments. In addition to knowledge sharing, increased coordination among partners is another critical benefit of network activities. Effective coordination can simplify processes and

7.4. Networking for Global Startups

increase entry speed into new markets. Also, resolving conflicts within business networks means companies can more effectively deal with upcoming challenges and maintain stable relationships with partners and customers. This coordination and conflict resolution type ultimately helps improve international investments' performance. It can lead to the sustainable growth and development of companies in the global arena. Therefore, networking activities not only help to improve the knowledge and skills of entrepreneurs and companies but also serve as a strategic tool to strengthen business positions internationally. This perspective allows companies to actively identify and acquire new opportunities using their networks and achieve success in the global competitive environment (Ripollés and Blesa, 2022).

International networking plays a crucial role in accelerating new investments and gaining a competitive advantage in the global arena. This process allows entrepreneurs and companies to access global markets more quickly and benefit from the various advantages these markets offer. Using existing networks, entrepreneurs can access multiple resources, including capital, technical know-how, and expertise in specific areas that may not be readily available within their home country. In addition to access to resources, international networking allows entrepreneurs to tap into the experiences and knowledge of others worldwide, which can help them better understand the challenges and opportunities in international markets. Also, interacting with diverse cultures and markets helps entrepreneurs to customize and adapt their strategies more effectively. Finally, international networking can help foster the growth and success of entrepreneurs on an international scale. This process provides new opportunities for business partnerships and international collaborations by establishing strategic and sustainable connections, which can lead to increased profitability and long-term success (Leite et al., 2016; Setti, 2023).

Competence in networking is critical for organizations in countries that rely heavily on international trade, such as Finland. These countries often strongly emphasize the importance and value of networking due to their limited domestic market size and the need to access larger markets. Effective networking allows organizations to acquire the resources and know-how they need, enabling them to collaborate with global business partners and accelerate economic and technological development. Strong communication skills would allow entrepreneurs to communicate effectively with various international stakeholders, including customers, investors, suppliers, and strategic partners. These skills help entrepreneurs understand and respond to global markets and cultures' different needs and expectations, ultimately establishing and maintaining solid and beneficial business relationships. Therefore, developing and strengthening international networking and communication skills is not only necessary for the individual success of entrepreneurs but also crucial for advancing the business and strategic goals of organizations in the global market. These skills are the main components of any successful international strategy and must be continuously strengthened and improved (Kokkonen and Koponen, 2020; Pronina, 2015).

7.5 Digital Entrepreneurship

The digital revolution, which has been in swing since the 1970s at least, and which gathered speed in the 1990s with the world web, has become central to entrepreneurship (Etemad *et al.*, 2010) and matured beyond imagination as technology continues to emerge. Digital entrepreneurship has significantly transformed access to international markets for small and medium enterprises (SMEs). The use of digital platforms and technologies enables SMEs to access global markets without the need for heavy investments or physical offices abroad. Online platforms such as e-commerce websites, social networks, and other digital tools allow businesses to market their products and services globally and attract new customers. In addition, digital technologies help entrepreneurs communicate more effectively with business partners and customers and better understand market needs and behaviors using big data and advanced analytics. This information allows SMEs to adapt their products or services based on the specific demands of each market, providing increased efficiency and improved customer experience. These abilities have enabled SMEs to enter new markets faster and more flexibly than before and compete with their larger competitors. Therefore, digital entrepreneurship has destroyed geographical boundaries and created countless opportunities for innovation and growth in the international arena (Walton, 2022).

The digital readiness of an economy is critical because it can significantly affect the country's ability to use new technologies and support innovations. This readiness is vital in directing national resources such as research and development to effectively support innovative entrepreneurship and small and medium enterprises (SMEs) in global markets. Due to the rapid growth of technology and the digitization of markets, economies that invest in developing digital infrastructure and empowering their workforce to use these technologies can enjoy significant benefits. This includes better access to international markets, competing with larger companies, and exploiting new global opportunities. In addition, digital readiness helps entrepreneurs and SMEs use new technologies such as big data, artificial intelligence, and the Internet of Things to improve processes, increase efficiency, and offer more innovative products and services. Also, digitizing processes can help reduce costs and provide access to more accurate data that can be used for strategic decisions. Ultimately, economies that invest in digital readiness will be more innovative and dynamic and able to be recognized as technology leaders on the global stage. These investments help strengthen the national economy and provide the necessary foundations for sustainable growth and development worldwide (Moeini Gharagozloo et al., 2022).

7.6 Digitalization: A Catalyst for Internationalization of SMEs

Digitalization is a powerful driving force for the internationalization of tiny and medium-sized companies. Studies show that increasing digital orientation allows companies to operate more quickly and efficiently in global markets. This process is influenced by several factors, including entrepreneur characteristics, product characteristics, company structure, technologies used, and market characteristics. Digitization allows companies to enjoy benefits such as more accessible access to market information, improvements in distribution and marketing channels, and increased speed of response to market changes. For example, online platforms and digital tools can help businesses better identify and engage with their international customers and provide customized services based on the needs of different customers. In addition, digitalization allows entrepreneurs to make more accurate strategic decisions using big data and advanced analytics. This helps them identify new market opportunities and manage their resources more effectively. As a result, digitalization not only increases the ability of companies to compete globally but also enables them to manage global markets efficiently and effectively (Lee *et al.*, 2022; Song and Wu, 2021).

Digital platforms mentioned in Athens play a significant role in facilitating the global expansion of SMEs, especially with the possibilities they provide to cross linguistic and cultural boundaries. These platforms allow companies to operate in diverse markets and not only be limited to English-speaking markets but also enter multilingual and culturally diverse markets. Automatic translation tools and multilingual interactive solutions help companies offer their websites, applications, and digital content in different languages. This enables better access and understanding of products and services for customers worldwide and enables companies to communicate with a broader range of audiences. In addition, digital platforms allow companies to optimize their marketing and sales strategies by better understanding different cultures. By analyzing data collected from other markets, companies can better understand consumer preferences and needs in other markets and design their products or services accordingly. Therefore, digital platforms not only provide new opportunities for the growth and expansion of companies in international markets but also help them to operate more successfully and effectively in multicultural environments (Reuber *et al.*, 2022).

To conclude, Section 7 explores important and emerging topics in international entrepreneurship, focusing specifically on how small and medium-sized enterprises (SMEs) internationalize, the emergence of global startups, and digital entrepreneurship. This section shows how these factors shape global business environments and make international markets more accessible.

The internationalization of SMEs is highlighted as a crucial process that enables them to reduce trade barriers and access global markets

7.6. Digitalization: A Catalyst for Internationalization of SMEs

using digital technologies and e-commerce platforms. Global startups begin with a worldwide vision and use innovative technologies to accelerate their international growth. Additionally, digital entrepreneurship allows companies to effectively communicate with global audiences through tools like social networks and online platforms.

This section demonstrates that international entrepreneurship provides insights into expanding businesses across borders and reflects broader socio-economic trends influencing global business strategies. Future research in this field is expected to explore these issues further, uncover new insights, and guide entrepreneurs and policymakers in navigating the complex landscape of international trade.

8

Toward the Future

As a dynamic and scholarly field, international entrepreneurship faces diverse and widespread changes shaped by technological, social, and economic global developments. This section attempts to provoke thought for future research.

Advanced technologies such as artificial intelligence, blockchain, and the Internet of Things (IoT) are crucial in shaping new business models. These technologies offer entrepreneurs opportunities to explore new markets and connect with customers more effectively quickly. Furthermore, demographic shifts and urbanization trends impact consumer demand and preferences, creating a foundation for new entrepreneurial opportunities in international markets. The analyses in this section help readers identify opportunities that stem from migration and the role of entrepreneurs, who can act as bridges between cultures and markets. Additionally, the growing importance of sustainability and social responsibility, particularly among younger generations, will significantly shape entrepreneurial directions.

Through a detailed analysis of the impacts and dependencies of these factors, this last section offers thought-provoking perspectives and practical strategies to respond to global developments. Here, we strive to provide a scientific roadmap for a better and deeper understanding of international entrepreneurship trends, helping entrepreneurs operate more effectively in dynamic global environments.

8.1 Examining the Drivers

In understanding and comprehending international entrepreneurship as an academic field, examining and analyzing the factors affecting it is of great importance. Introducing and analyzing these factors aims to identify better and understand the key drivers that can influence the success or failure of international entrepreneurs. Drivers are factors that affect the directions and future trends of global entrepreneurship. Their precise identification allows entrepreneurs to conduct more accurate strategic planning and respond to new opportunities with greater preparedness.

These drivers have been gathered based on studies and precise analyses of theorists in the field. These drivers are introduced in the form of structural and systematic analysis, not only to examine their direct impact on international entrepreneurship but also to consider how they influence and influence each other. This approach provides a deeper understanding of the complexities and challenges entrepreneurs face on an international stage and helps them compete more effectively in the global market with better strategies.

Therefore, analyzing and introducing these twelve drivers is essential for the current understanding of international entrepreneurship and preparing and guiding entrepreneurs to face future developments. This more profound knowledge and experience enable the prediction of future trends and the adjustment of effective strategies in response to them, strengthening the competitive position of entrepreneurs on a global scale.

The definition of each of the drivers will be provided as follows:

(1) Technological Disruption: Technologies that disrupt existing markets create new opportunities for international entrepreneurs. Innovations such as artificial intelligence, blockchain, and the Internet of Things (IoT) open new sectors for business. They can

8.1. Examining the Drivers

redefine mechanisms for new competitive strategies and enable dialogue and collaboration with other countries.

(2) Demographic Shifts: Demographic changes, such as aging populations in developed countries and younger populations in emerging markets, affect market needs and consumer behaviors, setting the stage for entrepreneurial opportunities on an international scale for suitable products and services.

(3) Urbanization Trends: The boom in urbanization in many countries creates a higher concentration of potential customers and changes in lifestyle, which can influence the demand for necessary products and services. Urban centers can be defined as hubs of innovation, providing a favorable environment for entrepreneurial activities.

(4) Migration and Diaspora Entrepreneurs: Migrants often act as bridges between their home countries and host countries, facilitating international trade and entrepreneurship. Integrating different cultures can lay the groundwork for international industrial economic collaborations, enhancing the scope of global entrepreneurship.

(5) Digitalization and E-commerce Growth: The expansion of e-commerce and the emergence of digital platforms have transformed businesses and industries globally. Entrepreneurs can use these platforms to expand their operations internationally without needing physical stores. Additionally, digital platforms have standardized service levels, providing a structured satisfaction that identifies the needs and values of different global communities for business and industry owners.

(6) Sustainability and Social Responsibility: Sustainability and sustainable development have gained increasing importance over time, with society becoming more aware of their impact on environmental scenarios. The rise in consumer awareness about ecological and social issues has led to an increased demand for sustainable and ethical products. International entrepreneurs focusing on

sustainability can gain a competitive advantage and access new markets.

(7) Changes in Consumer Preferences: Global exposure through media and travel leads to the convergence of tastes and a tendency to offer diverse products. Entrepreneurs can capitalize on these evolving preferences by providing innovative products that cater to global audiences.

(8) Access to Venture Capital and Funding: The availability of financial resources, primarily from venture capital firms specialized in international growth, can significantly affect the ability of startups to expand abroad. Regions with active venture capital markets are often hotspots for global entrepreneurship.

(9) Political Stability and International Relations: The political climate of a country affects its attractiveness for investment and foreign entrepreneurship. Countries with stable governments and positive international relations are more likely to attract global entrepreneurs.

(10) Exchange Rate Volatility: Currency-value Fluctuations can affect business costs abroad. Entrepreneurs must manage exchange rate risks, mainly when their business models depend on importing or exporting goods.

(11) Intellectual Property Protection: Effective legal frameworks for protecting intellectual property rights are crucial for technology and creative industries. Entrepreneurs are more inclined to invest in countries that legally protect their innovations.

(12) Global Supply Chains: The ability to manage and optimize supply chains internationally is a vital driver for businesses involved in manufacturing and distribution. Efficient supply chain management can lead to cost reductions and faster market entry.

8.2 Using MicMac Software in the Analysis of International Entrepreneurship: Integrating Expert and Entrepreneur Perspectives

Utilizing MicMac software for the analysis of international entrepreneurship is a targeted choice. This software, part of the suite of tools for structural analysis in future studies, allows us to measure and analyze the direct and indirect impacts of various factors within a complex system. MicMac is beneficial because it can identify key drivers and constraints that may affect international entrepreneurship. This software is particularly useful in determining the influence and interdependence of factors, formulating effective strategies, and better understanding the challenges and opportunities ahead.

In using this software, we have benefited from the opinions and insights of international entrepreneurs and experts in the field to ensure that the analyses are not only based on theoretical data but also on authentic and actual experiences from the field of international entrepreneurship. This combined approach, involving data collection through surveys, interviews, and expert workshops, has helped us provide a comprehensive and valid analysis of the complexities of international entrepreneurship. Through these analyses, a consensus among experts and entrepreneurs is achieved, which aids in deepening insights and presenting an accurate picture of entrepreneurial activities globally.

The MicMac output table is valuable for analyzing factors' direct and indirect impact and dependence in a complex system. Table 8.1 shows the effects and dependencies of this specific case on international entrepreneurship. This data is invaluable for identifying key factors that should be considered in policymaking and decision-making. The following is a scientific and precise analysis of this table:

8.3 MicMac Analysis

(1) *Direct Impact and Dependence*

- Factors with the highest direct impact (D5, D7, D8, D12): These factors represent points of strength in the system that can change other system elements. For example, D5, which

Table 8.1: Assessment of direct and indirect dependencies of drivers

Rank	Label	Direct Influence	Label	Direct Dependence	Label	Indirect Influence	Label	Indirect Dependence
1	D5	1099	D5	1151	D5	1090	D5	1129
2	D7	1047	D7	1047	D7	1038	D7	1039
3	D8	942	D8	942	D12	959	D12	957
4	D12	942	D12	942	D8	913	D8	915
5	D1	890	D3	890	D1	912	D3	883
6	D3	837	D11	837	D11	855	D11	849
7	D11	837	D1	732	D3	834	D1	764
8	D4	732	D2	732	D6	749	D6	757
9	D6	732	D4	732	D4	725	D2	738
10	D2	680	D6	732	D2	690	D4	728
11	D9	680	D9	680	D9	649	D9	658
12	D10	575	D10	575	D10	580	D10	578

tops this list, can be crucial for adopting structural changes in entrepreneurship policies.

- Factors with the highest direct dependence (D5, D7, D8, D12): These factors also show the most significant dependence on other factors, meaning that changes in these factors can significantly affect other system elements.

(2) *Indirect Impact and Dependence*

- Factors with the highest indirect impact (D5, D7, D12, D8) can influence the system through indirect pathways. This highlights the importance of understanding hidden relationships in the system, which may not be apparent at first glance.
- Factors with the highest indirect dependence (D5, D7, D12, D8): The indirect dependencies of these factors indicate that they play a crucial role in the stability and overall functioning of the system. These dependencies can also reveal vulnerable points in the system.

8.4 Suggestions for Further Research

(1) Deeper Examination of Factors D5 and D7: Since these factors rank highly in all four sections of impact and dependence (direct and indirect), a more detailed study could better understand how they influence other factors and the overall system.

(2) Analysis of Dynamics Between Factors: Understanding how factors with high impact and dependence interact and the effect of these interactions on international entrepreneurship could help develop more effective strategies to enhance entrepreneurship.

(3) Using Scenario Modeling to Predict Possible Changes in the System: Given the known impact and dependence of factors, various scenarios can be modeled to predict the possible effects of changes in one or more factors on the system.

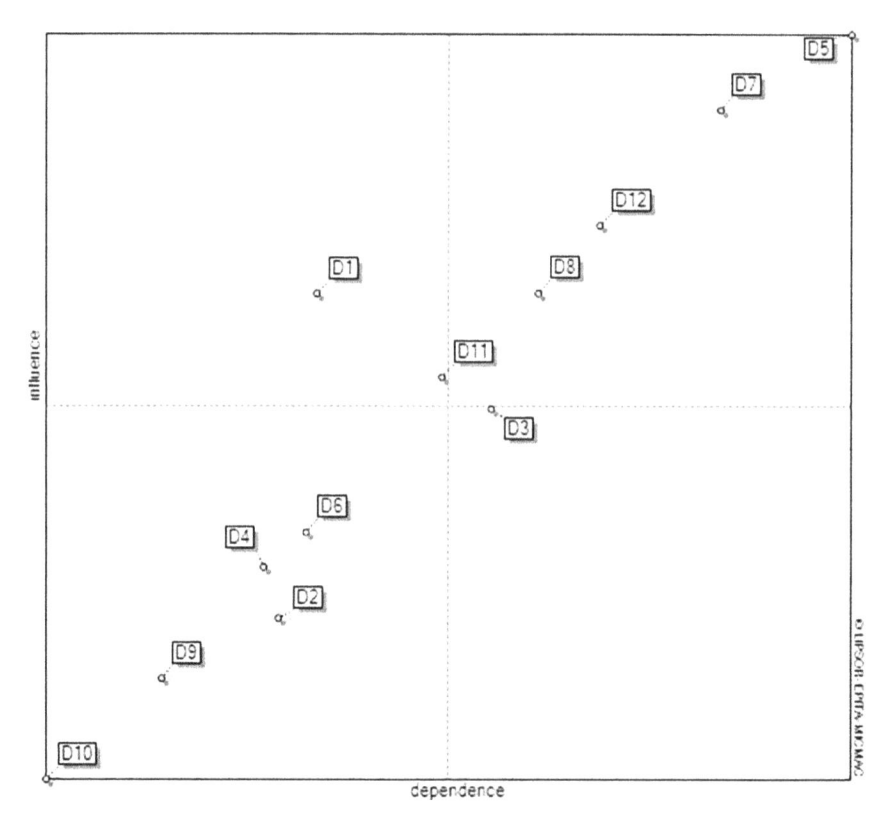

Figure 8.1: Indirect influence/dependence map.

Indirect Impact and Dependence Analysis: The indirect impact and dependence diagram obtained from the MicMac method is an efficient tool for structural analysis and determining critical factors in international entrepreneurship studies. The diagram in Figure 8.1 displays the positions of various aspects based on two main dimensions: impact and dependence. In this section, we proceed with a deeper scientific analysis of this diagram and the interplay of factors in international entrepreneurship.

8.5 Definition of Chart Dimensions

Impact represents the power of a factor to influence other aspects. Factors located at the top of the chart have a more substantial impact and are recognized as primary drivers in the system.

Dependency measures how much factors are influenced by other factors in the system. Factors positioned on the right side of the chart are highly dependent on different factors, and changes in these factors can have widespread effects on the entire system.

8.6 Analysis of Key Factors

(1) *Strong Driving Factors (D7 and D12):*

- D7 (Change in Consumer Preferences) and D12 (Global Supply Chains) are located at the upper right corner of the chart. This position indicates a high impact and significant dependency on these factors. They act as central elements in stimulating and advancing international entrepreneurial processes. Changes in consumer preferences may require redesigning products and services, and supply chains must continuously adapt to these changes.

(2) *Stable Factors (D11):*

- D11 (Support for Intellectual Property) is positioned at the center of the chart, indicating a balance between impact and dependency. This factor is stable, signifying its ongoing and continuous importance in the international entrepreneurship environment.

8.7 Examining Future Trends

Given the indirect impact and dependency map for various factors in international entrepreneurship, several key trends that will significantly affect this field in the future can be further and more deeply examined. Below, each of these factors and their mutual impacts on international entrepreneurship are explained:

(1) Digitalization and E-commerce (D5): Digitalization has caused a significant transformation in how businesses operate. With the expansion of information and communication technologies, geographical boundaries are becoming less of an obstacle for businesses. This factor allows entrepreneurs to access more global markets with less investment. Emerging technologies such as artificial intelligence and blockchain enable entrepreneurs to automate business processes, gather more accurate data, and improve customer experiences. Research has shown that entrepreneurs who use digital platforms for marketing and selling their products can more quickly reach international markets and gain a larger market share.

(2) Change in Consumer Preferences (D7): In today's rapidly changing world, consumer preferences are also evolving quickly, influenced by factors such as culture, economics, and technology. Entrepreneurs must continuously analyze markets and respond rapidly to changes to remain competitive. Research in consumer behavior shows that companies that customize their products according to local needs and preferences usually succeed more in international markets.

(3) Global Supply Chains (D12): Supply chains play a vital role in international entrepreneurship. The complexities of managing international supply chains and their impacts on entrepreneurship cannot be overlooked. Entrepreneurs must manage their supply chains using new technologies and forming strategic partnerships. Studies have shown that companies using advanced technologies like artificial intelligence and automation in their supply chain management have better abilities to reduce costs and increase efficiency.

(4) Access to Capital and Financing (D8): Access to financial resources is one of the biggest challenges for entrepreneurs, especially in the early stages of business development. International entrepreneurs should seek innovative financing sources, including venture capital, crowdfunding, and strategic partnerships. Research has indicated that startups with access to global investor networks significantly increase their sustainability and growth.

8.8. Potential Indirect Impacts Chart

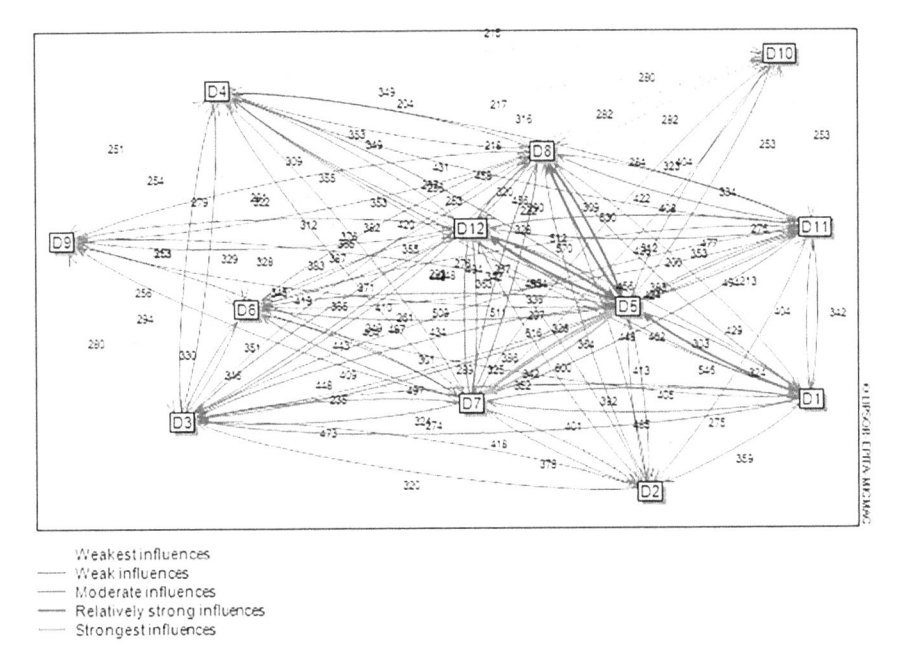

Figure 8.2: Potential indirect influence graph.

8.8 Potential Indirect Impacts Chart

The potential indirect impacts chart obtained from the MicMac method is a complex and practical analytical tool for examining and profoundly understanding the interactions between various factors in international entrepreneurship. This chart facilitates the visualization of a network of relationships and mutual impacts between different factors, each of which can influence or be influenced by the others (Figure 8.2). In what follows, we provide a detailed analysis of this chart and highlight key points for use in a scientific article.

8.9 Specialized Analysis and Highlights

(1) Factors D8 and D3:

- The strong impact of D8 (Access to Capital and Financing) on D3 (Urbanization Trends) highlights the importance of financing in urban development and entrepreneurial opportunities in urban areas. This topic could be central to further research on the impact of substantial financial investments on urban transformations.

(2) Factors D12 and D7:

- The strong relationship between D12 (Global Supply Chains) and D7 (Change in Consumer Preferences) demonstrates how changes in consumer demand can affect supply chains and increase the need for greater flexibility in supply chains.

(3) Impact Centers:

- D8 and D11 (Support for Intellectual Property) are impact centers in the chart, indicating their crucial role in stimulating entrepreneurial activities. These factors should be considered in policy-making and strategic planning.

8.10 Important Considerations in Research Processing

- Research on the Impact of Financial Policies on Urban Entrepreneurship: Examining how financing policies affect the development of entrepreneurship in urban areas and their connection to urbanization trends.

- Study on the Impact of Consumer Changes on Global Supply Chains: Conducting a more detailed analysis of how supply chains respond to rapid changes in the market and consumer preferences.

This analysis shows how MicMac impact and dependency charts can serve as powerful tools for better understanding the complex interactions

8.10. Important Considerations in Research Processing

within international entrepreneurial ecosystems and form a basis for formulating efficient and effective policies in this area.

To conclude, this section presents an extensive analysis of future trends and the direct and indirect impacts of various factors on international entrepreneurship. MicMac software in this analysis has enabled us to identify critical drivers such as technological changes, digitalization, sustainability, and social responsibility and examine their effects on the globalization of businesses. These drivers, carefully assessed by entrepreneurs and experts in the field, play a crucial role in shaping global business environments and provide new opportunities for innovation and growth for entrepreneurs.

The analyses in this section lead to a deeper understanding of how these factors influence entrepreneurship and strategies to address upcoming challenges. This understanding can serve as a valuable resource for future decision-making and the development of comprehensive policies at the global level.

References

Aceytuno, M. T., C. Sánchez-López, and M. A. de Paz-Báñez (2020). "Rising inequality and entrepreneurship during economic downturn: An analysis of opportunity and necessity entrepreneurship in Spain". *Sustainability*. 12(11). DOI: 10.3390/su12114540.

Ács, Z. J. and D. B. Audretsch (Eds.) (1991). *Innovation and Technological Change: An International Comparison*. University of Michigan Press.

Acs, Z., L. P. Dana, and M. Jones (2003). "Toward new horizons: The internationalisation of entrepreneurship". *Journal of International Entrepreneurship*. 1(1): 5–12.

Ajayi-Nifise, A. O., S. T. Tula, O. F. Asuzu, N. Z. Mhlongo, F. O. Olatoye, and C. V. Ibeh (2024). "The role of government policy in fostering entrepreneurship: A USA and Africa review". *International Journal of Management & Entrepreneurship Research*. 6(2): 352–367.

Alon, I., M. Lerner, and A. Shoham (2016). "Cross-national cultural values and nascent entrepreneurship: Factual versus normative values". *International Journal of Cross Cultural Management*. 16(3): 321–340.

Anglin, A. H., M. T. Wolfe, J. C. Short, A. F. McKenny, and R. J. Pidduck (2018). "Narcissistic rhetoric and crowdfunding performance: A social role theory perspective". *Journal of Business Venturing*. 33(6): 780–812.

Annushkina, O. E. and A. Regazzo (2020). "Strategic decisions in international business". In: *The Art of Going Global*. Cham: Palgrave Macmillan. DOI: 10.1007/978-3-030-21044-1_7.

Anwar, M., S. Li, A. Al-Omush, and M. Al-Nimer (2023). "SMEs' internationalization: Mapping the field through finance, ITC, and social ties". *Sustainability*. 15(4): 3162.

Audretsch, D. B., G. J. Castrogiovanni, D. Ribeiro, and S. Roig (2005). "Linking entrepreneurship and management: Welcome to the International Entrepreneurship and Management Journal". *The International Entrepreneurship and Management Journal*. 1: 5–7.

Audretsch, D. and E. Lehmann (2011). *Corporate Governance in Small and Medium-Sized Firms*. Edward Elgar Publishing.

Autio, E., G. George, and O. Alexy (2011). "International entrepreneurship and capability development-qualitative evidence and future research directions". *Entrepreneurship Theory and Practice*. 35(1): 11–37.

Bachmann, N., R. Rose, V. Maul, and K. Hölzle (2024). "What makes for future entrepreneurs? The role of digital competencies for entrepreneurial intention". *Journal of Business Research*. 174. DOI: 10.1016/j.jbusres.2023.114481.

Becker-Ritterspach, F., K. Lange, and J. Becker-Ritterspach (2017). "Divergent patterns in institutional entrepreneurship of MNCs in emerging economies". *Critical Perspectives on International Business*. 13(3): 186–203.

Bendell, B. L., D. M. Sullivan, and K. J. Hanek (2020). "Gender, technology and decision-making: Insights from an experimental conjoint analysis". *International Journal of Entrepreneurial Behaviour and Research*. 26(4): 647–670.

Blais, R. A. and J. M. Toulouse (1990). "National, regional or world patterns of entrepreneurial motivation? An empirical study of 2,278 entrepreneurs and 1,733 non-entrepreneurs in fourteen countries on four continents". *Journal of Small Business & Entrepreneurship.* 7(2): 3–20.

Boggio, C., F. Coda Moscarola, and A. Gallice (2020). "What is good for the goose is good for the gander?: How gender-specific conceptual frames affect financial participation and decision-making: What is good for the goose is good for the gander?" *Economics of Education Review.* 75. DOI: 10.1016/j.econedurev.2019.101952.

Bolzani, D. and M. D. Foo (2018). "The 'why' of international entrepreneurship: Uncovering entrepreneurs' personal values". *Small Business Economics.* 51: 639–666.

Böttcher, T. P., S. Empelmann, J. Weking, A. Hein, and H. Krcmar (2024). "Digital sustainable business models: Using digital technology to integrate ecological sustainability into the core of business models". *Information Systems Journal.* 34(3): 736–761.

Boustanifar, H., E. J. Zajac, and F. Zilja (2022). "Taking chances? The effect of CEO risk propensity on firms' risky internationalization decisions". *Journal of International Business Studies.* 1–24.

Broccardo, L., E. Truant, and L.-P. Dana (2023). "The interlink between digitalization, sustainability, and performance: An Italian context". *Journal of Business Research.* 158: 113621. DOI: 10.1016/j.jbusres.2022.113621.

Bruton, G., C. Sutter, and A. K. Lenz (2021). "Economic inequality – Is entrepreneurship the cause or the solution? A review and research agenda for emerging economies". *Journal of Business Venturing.* 36(3). DOI: 10.1016/j.jbusvent.2021.106095.

Busenitz, L. W. (1999). "Entrepreneurial risk and strategic decision making: It's a matter of perspective". *The Journal of Applied Behavioral Science.* 35(3): 325–340.

Cavusgil, S. T. and G. Knight (2015). "The born global firm: An entrepreneurial and capabilities perspective on early and rapid internationalization". *Journal of International Business Studies.* 46: 3–16.

Chang, F. Y., R. Jack, and C. M. Webster (2017). "Pre and post-entry resource needs for international entrepreneurs: The role of government and industry networks". *Journal of Management & Organization.* 23(2): 186–205.

Chetty, S. and C. Campbell-Hunt (2003). "Paths to internationalisation among small-to medium-sized firms: A global versus regional approach". *European Journal of Marketing.* 37(5/6): 796–820.

Chopra, R., A. Agrawal, G. D. Sharma, A. Kallmuenzer, and L. Vasa (2024). "Uncovering the organizational, environmental, and socio-economic sustainability of digitization: Evidence from existing research". *Review of Managerial Science.* 18(2): 685–709.

Chowdhury, F. and D. B. Audretsch (2021). "Do corruption and regulations matter for home country nascent international entrepreneurship?" *The Journal of Technology Transfer.* 46: 720–759.

Cieślik, J. (2017). "International dimension of entrepreneurship". In: *Entrepreneurship in Emerging Economies.* Cham: Palgrave Macmillan. DOI: 10.1007/978-3-319-41721-9_7.

Cieślik, J. and J. Cieślik (2017). "International dimension of entrepreneurship". In: *Entrepreneurship in Emerging Economies: Enhancing Its Contribution to Socio-Economic Development.* 195–218.

Clark, D. R. and R. J. Pidduck (2023). "International new ventures: Beyond definitional debates to advancing the cornerstone of international entrepreneurship". *Journal of Small Business Management.* 62(3): 1549–1571.

Colli, A., E. García-Canal, and M. F. Guillén (2013). "Family character and international entrepreneurship: A historical comparison of Italian and Spanish 'new multinationals'". *Business History.* 55(1): 119–138.

Costa, S., A. J. Frederiks, P. D. Englis, B. G. Englis, and A. J. Groen (2023). "Global before birth: A study of internationalization mindsets of entrepreneurs". *Journal of the International Council for Small Business.* 4(2): 212–224.

Cowden, B., M. Karami, J. Tang, W. Ye, and S. Adomako (2023). "The gendered effects of effectuation". *Journal of Business Research.* 155. DOI: 10.1016/j.jbusres.2022.113403.

Crespo, N. F., C. F. Crespo, and G. M. Silva (2024). "Every cloud has a silver lining: The role of business digitalization and early internationalization strategies to overcome cloudy times". *Technological Forecasting and Social Change*. 200. DOI: 10.1016/j.techfore.2023.123084.

Cricelli, L. and S. Strazzullo (2021). "The economic aspect of digital sustainability: A systematic review". *Sustainability*. 13(15): 8241.

Cumming, D., M. Meoli, A. Rossi, and S. Vismara (2024). "ESG and crowdfunding platforms". *Journal of Business Venturing*. 39(1). DOI: 10.1016/j.jbusvent.2023.106362.

Cumming, D., H. J. Sapienza, D. S. Siegel, and M. Wright (2009). "International entrepreneurship: Managerial and policy implications". *Strategic Entrepreneurship Journal*. 3(4): 283–296.

Dai, L., V. Maksimov, B. A. Gilbert, and S. A. Fernhaber (2014). "Entrepreneurial orientation and international scope: The differential roles of innovativeness, proactiveness, and risk-taking". *Journal of Business Venturing*. 29(4): 511–524.

Dana, L. P. ed. (2004). *Handbook of Research on International Entrepreneurship*. Cheltenham, United Kingdom: Edward Elgar.

Dana, L. P. (2007). *International Handbook of Research on Indigenous Entrepreneurship*. Cheltenham, United Kingdom: Edward Elgar.

Dana, L. P. (2017). "International entrepreneurship research: How it evolved and directions for the future". *International Journal of Entrepreneurship & Small Business*. 30(4): 477–489.

Dana, L. P. (2018). *Entrepreneurship in Western Europe: A Contextual Perspective*. Singapore & London: World Scientific.

Dana, L. P., H. Etemad, and R. W. Wright (1999a). "Theoretical foundations of international entrepreneurship". In: *International Entrepreneurship: Globalization of Emerging Businesses*. Ed. by R. W. Wright. JAI Press. 3–22.

Dana, L. P., H. Etemad, and R. W. Wright (1999b). "The impact of globalization on SMEs". *Global Focus*. 11(4): 93–106.

Dana, L. P., H. Etemad, and R. W. Wright (2000). "The global reach of symbiotic networks". *Journal of Euromarketing*. 9(2): 1–16.

Dana, L. P., H. Etemad, and R. W. Wright (2013). "Toward a paradigm of symbiotic entrepreneurship". *International Journal of Entrepreneurship and Small Business*. 5(2): 109–126.

Dana, L. P., A. Salamzadeh, M. Hadizadeh, G. Heydari, and S. Shamsoddin (2022a). "Urban entrepreneurship and sustainable businesses in smart cities: Exploring the role of digital technologies". *Sustainable Technology and Entrepreneurship.* 1(2). DOI: 10.1016/j.stae.2022.100016.

Dana, L. P., A. Salamzadeh, S. Mortazavi, and M. Hadizadeh (2022b). "Investigating the impact of international markets and new digital technologies on business innovation in emerging markets". *Sustainability.* 14(2). DOI: 10.3390/su14020983.

Dana, L. P. and R. W. Wright (1997). "Toward the internationalization of entrepreneurship research". *Journal of International Business & Entrepreneurship.* 5(1): 1–26.

Dana, L. P. and R. W. Wright (2009). "International entrepreneurship: Research priorities for the future". *International Journal of Globalisation and Small Business.* 3(1): 90–134.

Danielsen, D. (2010). "Local rules and a global economy: An economic policy perspective". *Transnational Legal Theory.* 1(1): 49–115.

De Moortel, K., T. Crispeels, J. Xie, and Q. Jing (2021). "Do interpersonal networks mediate the relationship between international academic mobility and entrepreneurial knowledge?" *Minerva.* 1–27.

Dean, T. J. and J. S. McMullen (2007). "Toward a theory of sustainable entrepreneurship: Reducing environmental degradation through entrepreneurial action". *Journal of Business Venturing.* 22(1): 50–76.

Dewan, J. and A. K. Singh (2019). "Strategies and processes of internationalization: A case study of the KARAM group of companies". In: *Transnational Entrepreneurship. Entrepreneurship and Development in South.* Ed. by M. Manimala, K. Wasdani, and A. Vijaygopal. Asia, Singapore: Longitudinal Narratives. Springer. DOI: 10.1007/978-981-10-6298-8_8.

Dimitratos, P., T. Buck, M. Fletcher, and N. Li (2016). "The motivation of international entrepreneurship: The case of Chinese transnational entrepreneurs". *International Business Review.* 25(5): 1103–1113.

Dominguez, N. and M. Raïs (2012). "Risk-seeking behaviours in growth strategies of SMEs: Targeting unstable environments". In: *15th McGill International Entrepreneurship Conference.* 21.

Dy, A. M., S. Marlow, and L. Martin (2017). "A web of opportunity or the same old story? Women digital entrepreneurs and intersectionality theory". *Human Relations*. 70(3): 286–311.

Etemad, H. (2015). "The promise of a potential theoretical framework in international entrepreneurship: An entrepreneurial orientation-performance relation in internationalized context". *Journal of International Entrepreneurship*. 13: 89–95.

Etemad, H., C. Gurau, and L.-P. Dana (2022). "International entrepreneurship research agendas evolving: A longitudinal study using the Delphi method". *Journal of International Entrepreneurship*. 20(1): 29–51.

Etemad, H., I. Wilinson, and L.-P. Dana (2010). "Internetization as the necessary condition for internationalization in the newly emerging economy". *Journal of International Entrepreneurship*. 8(4): 319–342.

Etemad, H., R. W. Wright, and L.-P. Dana (2001). "Symbiotic international business networks: Collaboration between small and large firms". *Thunderbird International Business Review*. 43(4): 481–499.

Fernandes, C., P. M. Veiga, and S. Gerschewski (2023). "SME internationalisation: Past, present and future trends". *Journal of Organizational Change Management*. 36(1): 144–161.

Flores, O. G. (2022). "Topic modeling: The use of machine learning and reference management systems in the area of internationalization of small and medium enterprises (SMES)". *Modern Management Review*. 27(4): 7–17.

Franco-Leal, N. and R. Diaz-Carrion (2022). "How financing and information drive international corporate entrepreneurs' innovations". *Journal of International Entrepreneurship*. 20(2): 316–343.

Freeman, S., Y. Zhu, and M. Warner (2020). *International Entrepreneurship: A Comparative Analysis*. London: Routledge. DOI: 10.4324/9781351109673.

Frydrych, D., A. J. Bock, T. Kinder, and B. Koeck (2014). "Exploring entrepreneurial legitimacy in reward-based crowdfunding". *Venture Capital*. 16(3): 247–269.

Fuentelsaz, L., J. P. Maicas, and J. Montero (2022). "Do you need to be risk-tolerant to become an entrepreneur? The importance of the reference point". *Entrepreneurship Research Journal*. 12(4): 471–500.

Fuerst, S., O. Sanchez-Dominguez, and M. A. Rodriguez-Montes (2023). "The role of digital technology within the business model of sustainable entrepreneurship". *Sustainability*. 15(14): 10923.

Gabaix, X., J.-M. Lasry, P.-L. Lions, and B. Moll (2016). "The dynamics of inequality". *Econometrica*. 84(6): 2071–2111.

Genkova, P. (2016). "Experience abroad and its relation to intercultural competence and cross-cultural tolerance". *International Journal of Business and Management*. 11(5): 1.

Glavas, C. and S. Mathews (2014). "How international entrepreneurship characteristics influence Internet capabilities for the international business processes of the firm". *International Business Review*. 23(1): 228–245.

Gregori, P. and P. Holzmann (2020). "Digital sustainable entrepreneurship: A business model perspective on embedding digital technologies for social and environmental value creation". *Journal of Cleaner Production*. 272. DOI: 10.1016/j.jclepro.2020.122817.

Guo, Z. and W. Jiang (2020). "Risk-taking for entrepreneurial new entry: Risk-taking dimensions and contingencies". *International Entrepreneurship and Management Journal*. 16: 739–781.

Gupta, V. K., A. B. Goktan, and G. Gunay (2014). "Gender differences in evaluation of new business opportunity: A stereotype threat perspective". *Journal of Business Venturing*. 29(2): 273–288.

Gupta, V. K., D. B. Turban, S. A. Wasti, and A. Sikdar (2009). "The role of gender stereotypes in perceptions of entrepreneurs and intentions to become an entrepreneur".

Hagen, B., S. Denicolai, and A. Zucchella (2014). "International entrepreneurship at the crossroads between innovation and internationalization". *Journal of International Entrepreneurship*. 12: 111–114.

Halvarsson, D., M. Korpi, and K. Wennberg (2018). "Entrepreneurship and income inequality". *Journal of Economic Behavior and Organization*. 145: 275–293. DOI: 10.1016/j.jebo.2017.11.003.

References

Hassan, M. U. and A. Ayub (2019). "Women's experience of perceived uncertainty: Insights from emotional intelligence". *Gender in Management.* 34(5): 366–383.

Hisrich, R. D. (2015). *International Entrepreneurship: Starting, Developing, and Managing a Global Venture.* Sage Publications.

Holzmann, P. and P. Gregori (2023). "The promise of digital technologies for sustainable entrepreneurship: A systematic literature review and research agenda". *International Journal of Information Management.* 68: 102593. DOI: 10.1016/j.ijinfomgt.2022.102593.

Hosseini, M., H. Dadfar, and S. Brege (2018). "Firm-level entrepreneurship and international performance: A simultaneous examination of orientation and action". *Journal of International Entrepreneurship.* 16(3): 338–368.

Huang, K. G., N. Jia, and Y. Ge (2024). "Forced to innovate? Consequences of United States' anti-dumping sanctions on innovations of Chinese exporters". *Research Policy.* 53(1). DOI: 10.1016/j.respol.2023.104899.

Huo, H., C. Wang, C. Han, M. Yang, and W. L. Shang (2024). "Risk disclosure and entrepreneurial resource acquisition in crowdfunding digital platforms: Evidence from digital technology ventures". *Information Processing and Management.* 61(3). DOI: 10.1016/j.ipm.2024.103655.

Jafari-Sadeghi, V., H. Amoozad Mahdiraji, A. Devalle, and A. C. Pellicelli (2022). "Somebody is hiding something: Disentangling interpersonal level drivers and consequences of knowledge hiding in international entrepreneurial firms". *Journal of Business Research.* 139: 383–396. DOI: 10.1016/j.jbusres.2021.09.068.

Jafari-Sadeghi, V., S. Kimiagari, and P. P. Biancone (2020a). "Level of education and knowledge, foresight competency and international entrepreneurship: A study of human capital determinants in the European countries". *European Business Review.* 32(1): 46–68.

Jafari-Sadeghi, V., J. M. Nkongolo-Bakenda, L. P. Dana, R. B. Anderson, and P. P. Biancone (2020b). "Home country institutional context and entrepreneurial internationalization: The significance of human capital attributes". *Journal of International Entrepreneurship.* 18(2): 165–195.

Jafari-Sadeghi, V., A. Sukumar, E. Pagán-Castaño, and L. P. Dana (2021). "What drives women towards domestic vs. international business venturing? An empirical analysis in emerging markets". *Journal of Business Research*. 134: 647–660. DOI: 10.1016/j.jbusres.2021.05.055.

Javadian, G., M. Figueroa-Armijos, V. K. Gupta, M. Modarresi, and C. Dobratz (2021). "Does it pay to act feminine? A cross-cultural study of gender stereotype endorsement and cognitive legitimacy in the evaluation of new ventures". *International Journal of Gender and Entrepreneurship*. 13(4): 330–352.

Johanson, J. and J. E. Vahlne (1977). "The internationalisation of the firm: A model of knowledge development and increasing foreign commitments". *Journal of International Business Studies*. 8(1).

Johansson, L. and M. Persson (2018). "Make way for the artificial intelligence train: A qualitative case study investigating the internationalization of Swedish AI firms, as well as the drivers and barriers affecting their process".

Jones, M. V. and L. Casulli (2014). "International entrepreneurship: Exploring the logic and utility of individual experience through comparative reasoning approaches". *Entrepreneurship Theory and Practice*. 38(1): 45–69.

Kah, S., S. O'Brien, S. Kok, and E. Gallagher (2022). "Entrepreneurial motivations, opportunities, and challenges: An international perspective". *Journal of African Business*. 23(2): 380–399.

Kamakura, W. A., M. A. Ramón-Jerónimo, and J. D. Vecino Gravel (2012). "A dynamic perspective to the internationalization of small-medium enterprises". *Journal of the Academy of Marketing Science*. 40: 236–251.

Kamberidou, I. (2020). "Distinguished women entrepreneurs in the digital economy and the multitasking whirlpool". *Journal of Innovation and Entrepreneurship*. 9(1). DOI: 10.1186/s13731-020-0114-y.

Kang, H. Y. (2022). "Technological engagement of women entrepreneurs on online digital platforms: Evidence from the Apple iOS App Store". *Technovation*. 114. DOI: 10.1016/j.technovation.2022.102522.

Kašperová, E. (2021). "Impairment (in)visibility and stigma: How disabled entrepreneurs gain legitimacy in mainstream and disability markets". *Entrepreneurship and Regional Development.* 33(9–10): 894–919.

Kelly, D. G. and M. McAdam (2022). "Scaffolding liminality: The lived experience of women entrepreneurs in digital spaces". *Technovation.* 118. DOI: 10.1016/j.technovation.2022.102537.

Keupp, M. M. and O. Gassmann (2009). "The past and the future of international entrepreneurship: A review and suggestions for developing the field". *Journal of Management.* 35(3): 600–633.

Khambhata, K. K. (2023). "Internationalization of small and medium-sized enterprises (SMEs) in emerging markets".

Khan, R. U., Y. Salamzadeh, S. Z. A. Shah, and M. Hussain (2021). "Factors affecting women entrepreneurs' success: A study of small- and medium-sized enterprises in emerging market of Pakistan". *Journal of Innovation and Entrepreneurship.* 10(1). DOI: 10.1186/s13731-021-00145-9.

Khoo, C., E. C. L. Yang, R. Y. Y. Tan, M. Alonso-Vazquez, C. Ricaurte-Quijano, M. Pécot, and D. Barahona-Canales (2023). "Opportunities and challenges of digital competencies for women tourism entrepreneurs in Latin America: A gendered perspective". *Journal of Sustainable Tourism.* DOI: 10.1080/09669582.2023.2189622.

Kiss, A. N., W. M. Danis, and S. T. Cavusgil (2012). "International entrepreneurship research in emerging economies: A critical review and research agenda". *Journal of Business Venturing.* 27(2): 266–290.

Knight, G. A. and P. W. Liesch (2016). "Internationalization: From incremental to born global". *Journal of World Business.* 51(1): 93–102.

Kokkonen, L. and J. Koponen (2020). "Entrepreneurs' interpersonal communication competence in networking". *Prologi: Puheviestinnän Vuosikirja.* 16(1).

Kuratko, D. F. (2012). "Corporate entrepreneurship". In: *Handbook on Organisational Entrepreneurship.* Edward Elgar. 226–241.

Landström, H. (2020). "The evolution of entrepreneurship as a scholarly field, foundations and trends® in entrepreneurship". 16(2): 65–243.

Lee, Y. Y., M. Falahat, and B. K. Sia (2022). "Digitalisation and internationalisation of SMEs in emerging markets". *International Journal of Entrepreneurship and Small Business.* 45(3): 334–354.

Leite, Y. V. P., W. F. A. de Moraes, and V. S. Salazar (2016). "Expressions of relationship networking in international entrepreneurship". *Journal of International Entrepreneurship.* 14: 213–238.

Lerner, J. (2002). "When bureaucrats meet entrepreneurs: The design of effectivepublic venture capital'programmes". *The Economic Journal.* 112(477): F73–F84.

Li, X. and J. Gammelgaard (2014). "An integrative model of internationalization strategies: The corporate entrepreneurship-institutional environment-regulatory focus (EIR) framework". *Critical Perspectives on International Business.* 10(3): 152–171.

Liesch, P. W., L. S. Welch, and P. J. Buckley (2011). "Risk and uncertainty in internationalisation and international entrepreneurship studies: Review and conceptual development". *Management International Review.* 51: 851–873.

Lippmann, S., A. Davis, and H. E. Aldrich (2005). "Entrepreneurship and inequality". *Research in the Sociology of Work.* 15: 3–31.

Liu, Y., T. Schøtt, and C. Zhang (2019). "Women's experiences of legitimacy, satisfaction and commitment as entrepreneurs: Embedded in gender hierarchy and networks in private and business spheres". *Entrepreneurship and Regional Development.* 31(3–4): 293–307.

Lopes, J. M., S. Gomes, J. Oliveira, and M. Oliveira (2022). "International open innovation strategies of firms in European Peripheral Regions". *Journal of Open Innovation: Technology, Market, and Complexity.* 8(1). DOI: 10.3390/joitmc8010007.

Luo, Y. and J. Bu (2018a). "Contextualizing international strategy by emerging market firms: A composition-based approach". *Journal of World Business.* 53(3): 337–355.

Luo, Y. and J. Bu (2018b). "When are emerging market multinationals more risk taking?" *Global Strategy Journal.* 8(4): 635–664.

Maciejewski, M. and K. Wach (2019). "International startups from Poland: Born global or born regional?" *Central European Management Journal.* 27: 60–83.

References

McDougall, P. (1989). "International vs. domestic entrepreneurship: New venture strategic behaviour and industry structure". *Journal of Business Venturing.* 4: 387–400.

McDougall, P. and B. Oviatt (2000). "International entrepreneurship: The intersection of two research paths". *Academy of Management Journal.* 43(5): 902–906.

McDougall-Covin, P., M. V. Jones, and M. G. Serapio (2014). "High-potential concepts, phenomena, and theories for the advancement of international entrepreneurship research". *Entrepreneurship Theory and Practice.* 38(1): 1–10.

Mehrez, A. (2019). "Investigating critical obstacles to entrepreneurship in emerging economies: A comparative study between males and females in Qatar". *Academy of Entrepreneurship Journal.* 25(1): 1–15.

Moeini Gharagozloo, M. M., F. Askarzadeh, and A. Moeini Gharagozloo (2022). "More power for international entrepreneurs: The effect of digital readiness of economies on channeling national R&D resources to entrepreneurship". *Journal of International Entrepreneurship.* 20(3): 474–502.

Muralidharan, E. and S. Pathak (2020). "Home country institutions and international entrepreneurship: A multi-level framework-institutions and international entrepreneurship". In: *Handbook of Research on Approaches to Alternative Entrepreneurship Opportunities.* IGI Global. 291–314.

Nambisan, S. (2017). "Digital entrepreneurship: Toward a digital technology perspective of entrepreneurship". *Entrepreneurship: Theory and Practice.* 41(6): 1029–1055.

Nave, E. and J. J. Ferreira (2022). "A systematic international entrepreneurship review and future research agenda". *Cross Cultural and Strategic Management.* 29(3): 639–674.

O'Cass, A. and J. Weerawardena (2009). "Examining the role of international entrepreneurship, innovation and international market performance in SME internationalisation". *European Journal of Marketing.* 43(11/12): 1325–1348.

Ongo Nkoa, B. E. and J. S. Song (2023). "How digital innovation affects women's entrepreneurship in Africa? An analysis of transmission channels". *International Journal of Entrepreneurship and Innovation.* DOI: 10.1177/14657503231162288.

Oviatt, B. M. and P. P. McDougall (1995). "Global start-ups: Entrepreneurs on a worldwide stage". *Academy of Management Perspectives.* 9(2): 30–43.

Oware, K. M., A. A. Iddrisu, T. Worae, and J. Ellah Adaletey (2022). "Female and environmental disclosure of family and non-family firms. Evidence from India". *Management Research Review.* 45(6): 760–780.

Packard, M. D. and P. L. Bylund (2018). "On the relationship between inequality and entrepreneurship". DOI: 10.1002/sej.1270.

Park, Y. W., Y. J. Park, Y. W. Park, and Y. J. Park (2021). "The core challenge of CSR in entrepreneurial ventures". In: *Corporate Social Responsibility and Entrepreneurship for Sustainability: Leading in the Era of Digital Transformation.* 1–9.

Peiris, I. K., M. E. Akoorie, and P. Sinha (2012). "International entrepreneurship: A critical analysis of studies in the past two decades and future directions for research". *Journal of International Entrepreneurship.* 10: 279–324.

Peng, M. W. (2003). "Institutional transitions and strategic choices". *Academy of Management Review.* 28(2): 275–296.

Pindado, E., S. Alarcón, M. Sánchez, and M. García Martínez (2023). "International entrepreneurship in Africa: The roles of institutional voids, entrepreneurial networks and gender". *Journal of Business Research.* 166. DOI: 10.1016/j.jbusres.2023.114109.

Prashantham, S. and C. Dhanaraj (2010). "The dynamic influence of social capital on the international growth of new ventures". *Journal of Management Studies.* 47(6): 967–994.

Prochotta, A., E. S. C. Berger, and A. Kuckertz (2022). "Aiming for legitimacy but perpetuating clichés-Social evaluations of the entrepreneurial identity". *Entrepreneurship and Regional Development.* 34(9–10): 807–827.

References

Pronina, M. (2015). "The role of network competence and international business competence in multinational corporations: Subsidiary perspective".

Pucik, V., I. Björkman, P. Evans, and G. K. Stahl (2023). *The Global Challenge: Managing People Across Borders*. Edward Elgar Publishing.

Rahman, M. S., M. E. Haque, M. S. I. Afrad, S. S. Hasan, and M. A. Rahman (2023). "Impact of mobile phone usage on empowerment of rural women entrepreneurs: Evidence from rural Bangladesh". *Heliyon*. 9(11). DOI: 10.1016/j.heliyon.2023.e21604.

Ramachandran, J., S. Mukherji, and M. Sud (2006). "Internationalization from emerging nations: Evidence of strategic entrepreneurship". *IIM Bangalore Research Paper*. (244).

Ramírez, C. P. and A. Levy (2022). "Network strategy for entrepreneurs". In: *Next Generation Entrepreneurship*. IntechOpen.

Ratten, V. (2022). "Corporate entrepreneurship". In: *Analyse, Ideate and Grow. Classroom Companion: Business*. Singapore: Springer. DOI: 10.1007/978-981-19-0890-3_2.

Ratten, V. (2023). "Digital platforms and transformational entrepreneurship during the COVID-19 crisis". *International Journal of Information Management*. 72. DOI: 10.1016/j.ijinfomgt.2022.102534.

Ratten, V., J. Álvarez-García, and M. De La Cruz Del Rio-Rama (2019). *Entrepreneurship, Innovation and Inequality Exploring Territorial Dynamics*. Routledge.

Reuber, A. R., E. Tippmann, and S. Monaghan (2022). "Digital entrepreneurship and localization". In: *Digital Entrepreneurship and the Global Economy*. Routledge. 64–76.

Rialp, A., J. M. Merigó, C. A. Cancino, and D. Urbano (2019). "Twenty-five years (1992–2016) of the International Business Review: A bibliometric overview". *International Business Review*. 28(6): 101587.

Ripollés, M. and A. Blesa (2022). "International new ventures' international performance: A matter of network entrepreneurial orientation and network management activities". *Management Research Review*. 45(1): 65–85.

Rippa, P. and G. Secundo (2019). "Digital academic entrepreneurship: The potential of digital technologies on academic entrepreneurship". *Technological Forecasting and Social Change*. 146: 900–911.

Rosário, A. and J. Dias (2022). "Sustainability and the digital transition: A literature review". *Sustainability*. 14(7): 4072.

Rutherford, M. W. and B. G. Nagy (2014). "Legitimacy and entrepreneurial behaviors".

Salamzadeh, A., L. P. Dana, P. Ebrahimi, M. Hadizadeh, and S. Mortazavi (2024). "Technological barriers to creating regional resilience in digital platform-based firms: Compound of performance sensitivity analysis and BIRCH algorithm". *Thunderbird International Business Review*. 66(2).

Salamzadeh, A., S. S. Mortazavi, and M. Hadizadeh (2022). *Social Media and Digital Technologies Among Pottery Makers and in the Sewing Sector*. 217–238. DOI: 10.1007/978-3-030-82303-0_13.

Sciascia, S., P. Mazzola, J. H. Astrachan, and T. M. Pieper (2012). "The role of family ownership in international entrepreneurship: Exploring nonlinear effects". *Small Business Economics*. 38(1): 15–31.

Sedziniauskiene, R. and J. Sekliuckiene (2020). "Entrepreneurial orientation and new venture performance: The moderating role of network types". *European Journal of International Management*. 14(5): 842–865.

Setti, J. (2023). "International Trade and its influence on startups development (based on the startup business media network) (Doctoral dissertation, Private Higher Educational Establishment-Institute "Ukrainian-American Concordia University")".

Shahid, Z. A. and L. Hallo (2019). "A network perspective on the intermittent internationalising experiences of emerging economy entrepreneurial SMEs". In: *International Entrepreneurship in Emerging Markets: Nature, Drivers, Barriers and Determinants*. Emerald Publishing Limited. 7–31.

Sharma, M., S. Joshi, and K. Govindan (2023). "Overcoming barriers to implement digital technologies to achieve sustainable production and consumption in the food sector: A circular economy perspective". *Sustainable Production and Consumption*. 39: 203–215. DOI: 10.1016/j.spc.2023.04.002.

References

Shinnar, R. S., O. Giacomin, and F. Janssen (2012). "Entrepreneurial perceptions and intentions: The role of gender and culture". *Entrepreneurship: Theory and Practice*. 36(3): 465–493.

Simarasl, N., P. Tabesh, T. P. Munyon, and Z. Marzban (2022). "Unveiled confidence: Exploring how institutional support enhances the entrepreneurial self-efficacy and performance of female entrepreneurs in constrained contexts". *European Management Journal*. DOI: 10.1016/j.emj.2022.07.003.

Singh, A. and S. Majumdar (2020). "Entrepreneurship: Nation as a context". In: *Methodological Issues in Social Entrepreneurship Knowledge and Practice*. Singapore: Springer. 199–222.

Song, D. and A. Wu (2021). "Pursuing international opportunities in a digitally enabled world". *Digital Entrepreneurship: Impact on Business and Society*. 265–281.

Stenholm, P. and U. Hytti (2014). "In search of legitimacy under institutional pressures: A case study of producer and entrepreneur farmer identities". *Journal of Rural Studies*. 35: 133–142. DOI: 10.1016/j.jrurstud.2014.05.001.

Suchman, M. C. (1995). "Managing legitimacy: Strategic and institutional approaches". *The Academy of Management Review*. 20(3): 571.

Sullivan Mort, G. and J. Weerawardena (2006). "Networking capability and international entrepreneurship: How networks function in Australian born global firms". *International Marketing Review*. 23(5): 549–572.

Sun, H., A. K. Pofoura, I. Adjei Mensah, L. Li, and M. Mohsin (2020). "The role of environmental entrepreneurship for sustainable development: Evidence from 35 countries in Sub-Saharan Africa". *Science of the Total Environment*. 741. DOI: 10.1016/j.scitotenv.2020.140132.

Szabó, R. Z., B. Szedmák, A. Tajti, and P. Bera (2023). "Environmental sustainability, digitalisation, and the entrepreneurial perception of distances as drivers of SMEs' internationalisation". *Sustainability*. 15(3): 2487.

Szirmai, A., W. Naudé, and M. Goedhuys (Eds.) (2011). *Entrepreneurship, Innovation, and Economic Development*. Oxford University Press.

Tarba, S. Y. and T. Almor (2018). "Guest editors' introduction: International entrepreneurial ventures: Implications for international management". *International Studies of Management & Organization.* 48(2): 137–139.

Verbeke, A. and L. Ciravegna (2018). "International entrepreneurship research versus international business research: A false dichotomy?" *Journal of International Business Studies.* 49: 387–394.

Vershinina, N., P. Rodgers, S. Tarba, Z. Khan, and P. Stokes (2020). "Gaining legitimacy through proactive stakeholder management: The experiences of high-tech women entrepreneurs in Russia". *Journal of Business Research.* 119: 111–121.

Vracheva, V. and I. Stoyneva (2020). "Does gender equality bridge or buffer the entrepreneurship gender gap? A cross-country investigation". *International Journal of Entrepreneurial Behavior & Research.* 26(8): 1827–1844.

Walton, N. (2022). "Digital platforms as entrepreneurial ecosystems and drivers of born-global SMEs in emerging economies". In: *International Entrepreneurship in Emerging Markets.* Routledge. 84–106.

Wang, F., M. Jin, J. Li, Y. Zhang, and J. Chen (2022). "Profound impact of economic openness and digital economy towards a sustainable development: A new look at RCEP economies". *Sustainability.* 14(21): 13922.

Wei, R. and C. Pardo (2022). "Artificial intelligence and SMEs: How can B2B SMEs leverage AI platforms to integrate AI technologies?" *Industrial Marketing Management.* 107: 466–483.

Weiermair, K. and M. Peters (1998). "The internationalization behaviour of small-and medium-sized service enterprises". *Asia Pacific Journal of Tourism Research.* 2(2): 1–14.

Welch, L. S. and R. Luostarinen (1988). "Internationalization: Evolution of a concept". *Journal of General Management.* 14(2): 34–55.

Werhane, P. H. (2012). "Globalization and its challenges for business and business ethics in the twenty-first century". *Business and Society Review.* 117(3): 383–405.

Wright, R. and L. P. Dana (2003). "Changing Paradigms of International Entrepreneurship Strategy". *Journal of International Entrepreneurship.* 1(1): 135–152. Reprinted in Benjamin M. Oviatt and Patricia Phillips McDougall, eds., International Entrepreneurship, Cheltenham, UK: Edward Elgar, 2007, pp. 131–148.

Xiao, D. and J. Su (2022). "Role of technological innovation in achieving social and environmental sustainability: Mediating roles of organizational innovation and digital entrepreneurship". *Frontiers in Public Health.* 10. DOI: 10.3389/fpubh.2022.850172.

Yang, M. M., T. Li, and Y. Wang (2020b). "What explains the degree of internationalization of early-stage entrepreneurial firms? A multilevel study on the joint effects of entrepreneurial self-efficacy, opportunity-motivated entrepreneurship, and home-country institutions". *Journal of World Business.* 55(6): 101114.

Yang, S., R. Kher, and S. L. Newbert (2020a). "What signals matter for social startups? It depends: The influence of gender role congruity on social impact accelerator selection decisions". *Journal of Business Venturing.* 35(2). DOI: 10.1016/j.jbusvent.2019.03.001.

Young, S., P. Dimitratos, and L. P. Dana (2003). "International entrepreneurship research: What scope for international business theories?" *Journal of International Entrepreneurship.* 1(1): 31–42.

Zahra, S. A., L. R. Newey, and Y. Li (2014). "On the frontiers: The implications of social entrepreneurship for international entrepreneurship". *Entrepreneurship Theory and Practice.* 38(1): 137–158.

Zamantılı Nayır, D. and R. S. Shinnar (2020). "How founders establish legitimacy: A narrative perspective on social entrepreneurs in a developing country context". *Social Enterprise Journal.* 16(3): 221–241.

Zelezny, L. C., P. P. Chua, and C. Aldrich (2000). "Elaborating on gender differences in environmentalism". *Journal of Social Issues.* 56(3): 443–457.

Zhang, M. M., C. J. Zhu, H. De Cieri, P. J. Dowling, and Z. Chen (2019). "A corporate entrepreneurship perspective of pre-entry strategies for internationalization: A case study of a Chinese business conglomerate". *Thunderbird International Business Review.* 61(2): 243–254.

Zhou, X., C. Ma, X. Su, L. Zhang, and W. Liu (2024). "Knowledge is power: The impact of entrepreneurship education on the international entrepreneurship performance". *The International Journal of Management Education.* 22(3): 101028.

Zhu, C. J., M. M. Zhang, P. J. Dowling, H. DeCieri, and Z. X. Chen (2014). "Corporate entrepreneurship and internationalization of emerging MNEs: The case of a Chinese MNE". In: *Academy of Management Proceedings (Vol. 2014, No. 1, p. 15086).* Briarcliff Manor, NY 10510: Academy of Management.

Ziyae, B. and M. R. Zali (2017). "The reinvigorating of international entrepreneurship by open innovation strategy for Iranian businesses". In: *Iranian Entrepreneurship: Deciphering the Entrepreneurial Ecosystem in Iran and in the Iranian Diaspora.* 289–294.

Milton Keynes UK
Ingram Content Group UK Ltd.
UKHW021344011224
451693UK00010B/741

9 781638 284581